WESTMINSTER WRITERS JOURNAL

2023 Edition

TO OUR READERS:

FIVE may be a small number, until it's the symbol of commitment over time. Then it is worthy of note and celebration. This year, 2023, we celebrate the FIFTH Edition of the *Westminster Writers Journal*. We celebrate the literary aspiration and talent of the eighty residents whose fiction, non-fiction, memoirs, and poems have entertained and illuminated our lives since the publication of the first Journal in the spring of 2020. We celebrate the editors, copy editors, publicity team, and art editors who translated the idea of a journal into reality. We celebrate Westminster leadership, associates, and residents, who all supported this endeavor. We celebrate what we have achieved, but we only pause to celebrate–the sixth edition awaits us.

On the Cover: *Variants* – digital art by resident William Schleuse (from *Westminster Artists 2023*)

Interior Design by James Woodrick

The *Westminster Writers Journal* is a publication of the Westminster Manor Residents' Association. Editorial Board: Co-Managing Editors: Lori Humphreys and Boyd Taylor; Associate Editor: Mike Roche; Copy Editor-In-Chief: William Schleuse; Copy Editors: Nancy Benson, Tony Durniak, Jan McInroy, and Phyllis Schenkkan; Format Editor: James Woodrick; Proof Reader: Richard Campbell; Publicity And Marketing Team: Team Leader: Lori Humphreys; Team Members: David Helfert, Kathy McIntyre, Mike Roche, and Marjorie Woo-Mobley.

TABLE OF CONTENTS

POETRY

NON-FICTION

FICTION

CONTRIBUTORS' NOTES

POETRY

Three Poems

Betsy Bouchard

Song

Wind rustles through the golden grain
In the field outside my window.
Wrens hustle in leaves still damp with rain
And vie for bugs in the meadow
Near the old oak.

Autumn's music is crisp and bright
But when the sun relents and goes
A harvest moon heaves into sight
And soon its tent of pale light glows
Through the old oak.

Now I remember the ones I lost
And the other ones who lost me.

Stillness seeps into the darkened haunt
Of the wrens, the wind, and the falling leaves
Of the old oak.

Wild Life

It was a festive moment, the delivery of
thirty young opossums in the lumbering black truck
from Wildlife Rescue.
Pink opossum-hands clutched
the wire doors of their kennels,
black eyes black as eternity peered
over bubblegum pink noses round as golf balls.
They appeared curious, even alert in a laid-back
opossum way.

Orphans of the storm, so to speak, refugees
from the highways and back yards
of our nervous cities, they grew up
in solicitous cages and timed feedings
and security from all
but their own true nature.

We drove them down to the creek at dusk, set the kennels
out at intervals, doors ajar so they could make their first flight to freedom
among the tall grasses and drying spring wildflowers
and in the shade of oaks and cedars. Nearby, the creek tumbled
over limestone.
Paradise in our eyes.

When they wouldn't leave their kennels, we shook them and then dumped them.
Perplexed, they didn't scamper off to shelter, but paused and sniffed
the grass, investigated a log, stared at us as if for directions.
There was no joy, no homecoming.
They stood in place like actors who have forgotten their lines,
shifting from side to side, looking back at us for a prompt.

We finally left them as dusk settled and it began to sprinkle.
As we drove off, they were still in their places.
They didn't seem grateful. They didn't seem worried about owls
or coyotes or feral hogs.
They simply were.

Night Songs

City music, night tunes
Bass growls
Of freight train
hauling dunes
of rain - washed limestone
dug from the bowels
of the Lazy R
and Double R
outfits, their bones
now dancing
to the subtle bounce
of wheel on steel.

Suddenly the soprano aria
of a siren
outta-the-way
outta-the-way
rips through the clatter
then fades in a matter
of moments, like a day
shades into dark
when the night music starts.

The Tall Man

Lexa Crane

Does anyone visit the tall man at
night? When with head tipped
back,
and soles firmly planted,
he stargazes the firmament.
He stands close enough to the
river,
so he can see the city lights if
looking downstream; across
the dam, over the bridges,
beyond the skyscrapers,
and on and on for miles.

And what's he looking for
during the day?
This tall man searches
the clouds,
the wind,
the rains.
He scans for the comfort of
company,
for threats,
for birds,
for planes.
For admiration
with its affirmation.

He reflects light, night and day
off his body – for his body
is clothed in pounded and
crushed aluminum…
a protective coating.
He shines hope everlasting.

"I am awed by you," I say.
 "Can you hear me way
up there?"

He continues to survey the
universe.
I am surprised by joy.
Tears flood over my smile.

My Knew Spellchecker

Paul R. Lehman

When I was in college my goal was quite clear:
I'd be a great author whom critics would cheer.
But one major obstacle stood in my way—
I never could spell what I wanted to say.

In grade fore my spelling did laughter evoke;
By grade ate my struggle became the class joke.
My teachers concerns they could know longer hied;
"Wurst I have scene," was the phrase one applied.

So as I grew up it began to appear
That eye mite have too follow an other career.
I had two brake free from the whole aye was inn,
Oar success as an author I never wood win.

Then won day eye happened too press a wrong key
And discovered a spell checker on my pea sea.
It was their in plane cite; it was easy two view.
It was they're awl along, butt four me it was gnu.

My please had been herd. It seamed that at last
Spelling mist aches were a thing of the passed.
Too insure that each draught is of errors quite free
I have only two clique the appropriate quay.

Each word that eye rite now aye no does exist;
My fears of miss spelling can now bee dismissed.

I'm certain today, as I stair at my screen,
Know errors are lurking their hidden, unseen.

Each frays I construct now I'm sure is a joule;
Eye no aye halve knot contravened any rule.
If I laps or I'm lacks there's a digital wrap
From my deer friend and teem mate, my spell-checking app.

This helpful tool freeze mi of every concern;
Theirs no doubt that fourth with hi honors aisle urn.
My suite, kindly checker makes writing a breeze;
I've lodes of free thyme now too dew as eye pleas.

My mined is a storehouse of tails to bee tolled,
Of damsels sew fare and of heroes sew bowled.
My skill has groan greatly, buy weak and bye our;
My stile sum fine day will bare fruit and will flour.

Yule not bee surprised that I toile daze and knights
Too billed epic stories that clime epic heights.
And each word must meat thee tuff standards applied
Bye my spell-checking aid that aye keep buy my sighed.

But writers knead readers two reed what they rite,
And I halve no fans at awl. That is my plight.
I mussed fined a weigh the vast public to reach,
Too in thrall and inn spire, two a muse and to teach.

Four every one nose that when all's said and dun
To right gives one joy, satisfaction, and fun.
Butt it's all so quite true, and it aught too be said,
It's a shear waist of time if yore work isn't red.

My checker poured over this new peace as well,
So yew can bee certain no errors hear dwell.
I've maid know miss steaks aye am proud two declare
(Ore at leased their are nun of which eye am a wear).

My rimes and my pros are both hart felt and knew;
With laughter and tiers there in fused threw and threw.
But despite they're grate merit eye note with regret
Knot won of my works has bin published as yet.

Aye send them too publishers distant and near,
Butt never a word of response dew I here.
Why nun are accepted I'm given know clue,
And eye haven't the foggiest notion. Have ewe?

The Cure

Randy Parker

My wife of 52 years died.
Our *one-flesh* was ripped apart.
I was left half-a-being and grievously depressed.
I prayed incessantly for solace and connection.
Yet I reached out to find a cure for my grief.
I exercised regularly and ate healthfully.
This regimen helped but was not the cure.
I sought out friends.
Former friends shunned single-me.
I searched for new friends.
I attended a new church and joined a Small Group.
Being with new friends helped but was not the cure.
I saw my physician.
She prescribed an antidepressant.
It helped but the medication was not the cure.
I joined a grief group for two and one-half years.
Empathizing with grieving others heightened my despair.
It provided no solace and was not the cure.
I saw a therapist for eight months.
She was skilled but more depressed than I.
Therapy was not the cure.
I joined a dating site for elders.
I dated one woman, but there was no chemistry and no cure.
All these efforts only yielded more frustration and emptiness.
Then the Covid pandemic ensued.
It heightened my fear, isolation, and despair.

In exasperation, I prayed boldly, specifically, and relentlessly,
"Dear Father, help me find a Christian woman about my age,
who is beautiful in spirit and countenance,
who is intelligent and loving, and
who has many interests in common with me."
After months of praying, I received a call from an old friend.
Her husband had died recently.
She invited me to a *picnicky* lunch in her Westminster apartment.
Sharing our grief led to shared love.
Love dispelled our grief.
Love is the cure.

Three Poems

William Schleuse

Bemused

I am amused and confused
by the contradictory meanings of bemused.

Cardinal

First it meant a turn in a fence,
Then a gate, then a hinge on which it turns,
Then important numbers, virtues, even prelates.
Then, the color of a prelate's hat—now the color names a bird.
From a hinge to a bird—is that absurd?
No, just a metaphor unheard.

Expectations

At 45 I'd reached most goals.
      still, life seemed pretty tough.
I've since learned that from 40s on,
      one's happiness trends up.

Now, I'm 90, and I find,
      somewhat to my surprise,
that life transcends spare parts and pains,
      and joy's still on the rise!

With memory prompts and Siri's help,
      I find most all I need,
to learn and thrive and enjoy life
      in ways that still succeed.

Sonnet in Praise of Oxalis

Joan Smith

That drought last summer scorched my front yard brown
As cardboard. Plants drooped and fell. They needed
Life water… which was rightly metered down.
While blazing heat burned trees, pale grass receded.
Then fruitful autumn rains burst wide and blessed
Dry ground. Slight stems grew up where none had been.
Now wing-shaped leaves with green-and-purple dressed
Trefoils…vivid pink blossom-cups are seen.
They open sunward and close for clouds or night.
Amazing gift…rare foliage and flowers.
My joy's in sharing such a verdant sight
And bulbs with friends who learn its gentle powers.
The patterned colors of this birdlike weed
Enchant with beauty – shy delight indeed.

Three Poems

Betty Tyslan

Interstate Interlude

Three oversize loads   each at least four car lengths
merge ahead where I want to go
 dump truck and cement mixer to the left
 all lanes bumper-to-bumper

  butterfly glides between van and s u v
  a low floater   this traffic observer
  destination in question
  the only beauty among behemoths

  wheels begin to turn
  attention rebounds to surroundings
  misled butterfly fades
  pace hastens with vehicle cocoons

No Fire-Breather

I write; dragonfly on index knuckle rides along.
It flies off, returns, and lights on legal pad.
Then, lured by rhythm, lands on hand for a few lines.

Slender body of blue
with black accessories
and oblong wing networks

sits on four thread-thin legs
atop four bulbous feet.

Close study frightens fly.
It moves to left shoulder,
but interest brings it back
to land on hand where it reads.

Delicate wings whisper approval and black eyes bulge
with astonishment and pride to see itself,
improbable protagonist of backyard writing.

A Catch

Kennedy Le, you may not remember me,
but I remember you and still have your fish
the trivet you made in woodshop
a project you didn't want.
I told you that your mother would
you didn't agree and insisted
on giving it to me.
I was pleased but felt guilty.

Fish lives on my counter
next to the microwave
out of water.
I think of you

NON-FICTION

GROWING UP ON AN ARMY BASE DURING WWII

Barbara Adams

I was born in 1940 at the post hospital, soon to be named Brooke Army Medical Center, at Fort Sam Houston in San Antonio, Texas. My parents were "away," so as an only child, I was staying with my maternal grandparents. My grandfather was a brigadier general and was post commander from 1940 to 1946. Our household consisted of five people: my grandfather, my grandmother, Cubello, Probst, and me. The most important to me was Jimmy Cubello, the Filipino sergeant who was our cook. Each day I was left in his care, and he was a kind and fatherly figure to me. I was allowed to spend time in the kitchen watching him prepare meals. He was the constant presence in my early life. There was an orderly, Probst, who was a private and did our household cleaning. He kept the house spotless. Surnames were used, and I addressed them as "Cubello" and "Probst." Occasionally, Uncle Bob joined our household, though he was usually away at Episcopal High boarding school in Virginia. When he came home for holidays, an otherwise dreary house came alive with excitement. I remember staring at an unadorned living room with no tree or decorations and feared there would be no Christmas at all, but when Uncle Bob arrived, a decorated tree appeared as if by magic. He was my mother's younger brother and the center of my grandparents' lives. I loved him because as a teenager he brought youthful vibrancy and laughter to our house.

Like our spotless house, my grandfather's car was always clean and shining despite its army olive drab finish. In place of a state license plate, a plate with a single star identified the car as being that of a brigadier general. Family members were not allowed to be driven in the government-issue car except under unusual circumstances. I remember one such occasion when, barely visible in the backseat, I was being driven and noticed soldiers and even junior officers saluting me as the car passed. I was quite taken with this sign of respect to me as a four- or five-year old. Of course, they were saluting the star, which was saluted in case the general himself was in the car.

My constant question to my grandparents and Cubello was "When are my mother and father coming back from their 'trip'?" "Soon" was the standard reply. There had been no notes, postcards, wires, or gifts from their travels—no communication at all. I longed for them and missed them terribly. I wondered if they had forgotten me.

Because the specter of war loomed, I had become fearful. On the parade ground, there were soldiers with weapons guarding German POWs who were "policing" the grounds. The sight of guards carrying large rifles and guarding prisoners caused me to be anxious.

I had not been allowed playmates in these young years. I have wondered, looking back, if perhaps that was because only young officers would have had children my age to play with; that would have been inappropriate according to the military command structure. Their playing with the granddaughter of the post commander might have been perceived as favoritism by the general toward a junior officer and his family. Eventually, when I was five, a post kindergarten was constructed so that I would have a place to start school. That kindergarten year was my introduction to other children.

On one occasion (it must have been a Sunday, Cubello's day off), my grandmother warned me that if I did not eat my French toast for breakfast, she would call the military police to take me to the stockade. After breakfast, I was sitting alone on the wooden name marker at the street and the military police pulled up in their jeep and tried to talk to me. *Oh, no! They've come for me,* I thought. My legs shook so hard that I could barely stand as the MPs approached me. I later learned that they had arranged with my grandfather to take me for a ride in the jeep. However, I was so shaken they had to abandon their plans and walk me to our front door. How could they have known that they had been used as threats by my grandmother?

My father's father, J. Duncan Elliott, was a colonel in the army; I called him "Duncan" instead of "Grandfather." He lived in Washington, DC, and because he had to make the trip by automobile, he visited Texas only once a year. I remember him as loving, hugging, playful, and warm. On one visit to Fort Sam Houston, he stayed at the officers club and said I could stay overnight with him in his room. Of course, I arose early and wanted to play. I woke him and learned that one must not awaken a war veteran suddenly because it is startling and disorienting. My touch frightened him, and he jumped as if on a battlefield. Nevertheless, he let me straddle his knees to ride and sway, eventually allowing me to tumble, while safely holding my hands. He played with me, which no one had ever done. I adored him. Neither custodial grandparent hugged or played with me. I will always treasure my grandfather Duncan's warmth and playfulness.

A memory that still delights me is that of the horse-drawn ice wagon that came by each week. It was a thrill for me to see the tall, muscular draught horse. In the 1940s, we had "ice boxes" instead of refrigerators, and ice was custom-cut for the size of the household ice box.

Despite his reserved demeanor, my mother's father was given the nickname "Sunny" while at West Point. He was a horseman who competed internationally for the US Army when he was a young lieutenant and captain. At Fort Sam Houston, he frequently rode for pleasure across the parade ground, stopping in front of our house. Occasionally, I was given permission to cross the street to greet him and pat the statuesque horse. I do not remember his ever dismounting or lifting me into the saddle with him.

I once was invited to see Sunny's office, which was across the parade ground from our house. On this visit, his aides showed me the "bugle" that awakened the troops with reveille each morning and played taps in the evening. It was a great disappointment to discover that instead of a live bugler there was a vinyl record on an old-fashioned record player that blasted the familiar notes over a loudspeaker throughout the post. To learn that this was an illusion was disheartening and made me cry. Now it is commonplace for buglers to have a device inside the instrument that plays the tune because there are not enough real musicians to play for funerals and military events.

On the post, the quarters faced the street where no cars were allowed to park. The effect was one of orderliness, safety, and visual attractiveness. There was an alley behind the houses, and cars drove down it to their assigned garages. I had a swing set in the backyard which I seldom used because it was not much fun to swing alone. In that same backyard, open and unfenced, there was a faux bois (false wood) birdbath. There were other examples of faux bois in San Antonio and this method of sculpture fascinated me.

One day a girl about my age was strolling down the alley with her mother. It was summer and we both had on smocked, short-sleeved cotton dresses. Her mother stopped to speak to my grandmother. I had never seen this child before, but, pointing at my grandmother, she said to me, "She's not your mother. Your mother and father are dead." I couldn't breathe! I was shocked and overwhelmed by the deceit of my grandparents, but what she said rang true and many things fell into place for me.

In our living room were two framed pictures—one of a wedding in which the attractive couple ducked under crossed sabers held by officers in navy whites and the other of a pretty brunette lady with flowers in her hair. In the past, when I had asked who they were, I had always been told, "Oh, they are just friends." Now I confronted my grandmother, who acknowledged that what the child had said was true: those pictures were of my parents, and indeed they were not coming back, as I had been told. I was stunned at my grandparents' lies and betrayal. The specific details of my parents' death were not discussed, and it would be decades before I would research my family history, aided by my grandfather Duncan's scrapbook. I hungered for the truth, no matter how difficult it might be.

I discovered that my young father, a navy lieutenant, flew reconnaissance in a Curtiss SOC-3 Seagull pontoon biplane in the Naval Battle of Casablanca. Morocco was a colony of France at this time; France had surrendered, after signing the armistice with Nazi Germany. The French Army under Charles de Gaulle supported the Allies, whereas the Vichy regime, which controlled Morocco, was "officially neutral" but obliged to resist any attempt by France's allies to seize French territory or equipment for use against Germany. The French Navy was fighting for Germany and the Nazis, which is why the United States was attacking them at Casablanca. In trying to educate myself about this naval battle, I read a chapter from the series *History of United States Naval Operations in World War II* by Samuel Eliot Morison. I began weeping when I noticed, at the bottom of one page, a footnote that read: "From a Tuscaloosa Action Report, Enclosure E: Lt. Jesse Duncan Elliott, Jr. [my father] pilot of a spotting plane of Tuscaloosa, states in his report 'We scored a hit on one destroyer, which hauled for the harbor smoking, and the *Brooklyn* split a destroyer in two.'" In a fifteen-volume history, the renowned naval historian of WWII quoted my young dad! What an extraordinary coincidence that I would see it!

From the air these planes could spot such activity as submarine presence, minefields, or the exchange of torpedoes, and credit could be given to one of our ships (or the enemy's) with a hit using color-coded ordnance. These spotting planes were catapulted into the air like a slingshot from a heavy cruiser ship. Upon return, the pontoons enabled the planes to taxi up alongside the ship; the top wing was hooked to a cable and winched aboard by a crane, and then the ship hoisted the planes aboard onto catapults once more.

The Allies won that important battle, and the ships, many of which had sustained torpedo damage, put into Boston Harbor and other US ports for refitting after the action. My mother was notified by wire at Fort Sam Houston that my father was on leave, and she took a coal-burning steam train to Boston to join him. It was Thanksgiving week and spirits were high.

When I was a young adult, two close friends had decided not to tell me that a book had recently been published with the title, *The Cocoanut Grove Fire.* But when I learned of it, read the book, and viewed the photographs, it was strangely freeing and healing for me finally to know about the devastating Boston Cocoanut Grove nightclub fire. In November of 1942 nearly five hundred people perished in the holocaust. Fifty-five servicemen died, and eleven children from five families were made orphans that night. I was one of those orphans. This tragedy would define me, and I would regard myself as an orphan for much of my life.

For a while it was a consolation to believe that my parents died in each other's arms, but the causes of death on their death certificates indicated otherwise. My father was identified by his Annapolis class ring. A fellow officer provided a uniform for his burial at Arlington National cemetery. Women were identified by hair color and scraps of fabric or surgeries and scars. Shoe size and personal effects were used in "sight recognition," as were shapes, proportions, and measurements. Families were discouraged, if not forbidden, from seeing the disfigured and burned bodies. My mother had with her an alligator purse that had been a wedding gift only three years earlier. This prized handbag helped to confirm her death.

In time I learned more inconceivable and horrific details about the tragedy. The license for the Grove allowed a maximum capacity of four hundred and sixty patrons, but there were more than a thousand in the Grove that night. There were more fatalities than the supper club's total capacity, and exits were locked or obscured by decorations to prevent anyone from trying to skip out on their bill. At the main entrance was a revolving door that was quickly jammed by the limbs of panicking patrons. Bodies were piled to the ceiling at every exit.

Firemen would have the same difficulty getting *into* the building as the occupants had getting *out* because the entire building was locked down and bolted. The fire department brought in twenty-five engine companies, a rescue company, five ladder companies, and a water tower.

The owner had once bragged that he didn't have to obey building codes because of his connections to the Boston mayor. After the fire and many formal inquiries, he finally went to prison for his flouting of codes and his shoddy remodeling practices. Years later, each victim was awarded $160 in compensation.

Another frightening memory from my early years emerged as we were on the way to Fort Sheridan, Illinois. This was my grandfather's last command before retiring because of disability. On the train I saw two uniformed young men with Asian features. In my six-year-old mind they were Japanese enemies and were going to kill me. I could not have understood that they were wearing our uniform and serving as Americans.

Living at Fort Sheridan was very different from living in Texas. I wore my first snowsuit there and built forts out of fall leaves, the smell of which remains with me. And there were ravines to play in. Lake Michigan was our "next-door neighbor" (our house "sided" directly on the lake) and the frozen lake made a particular thundering sound in winter. I attended Lake Forest Country Day School for first grade and was twice invited to have lunch at the home of a classmate. I was unaccustomed to having invitations to visit friends' homes and felt awkward. I had butterscotch pudding for the first time at one of these homes and found its taste to be quite exotic. I was not given to trying new foods and had to be coaxed to eat at all. A friend of my grandparents, Col. Reeves Rutledge, bought ice skates for me and took me down the steep bank to the frozen lake to teach me to skate. It was a kindness that has amazed me and stayed in my heart.

I remember Mrs. Douglas MacArthur coming to call on my grandmother. The two friends visited in a sitting room, and I was asked to wait outside the door where I could observe but not intrude. (Children were to be "seen but not heard.") Over her suit, Mrs. MacArthur wore a stone marten fur. It was complete with the heads of the animals with taxidermists' glass eyes, little black noses, and raised ears. One mouth bit the tail or a foot of the next, and the fur was draped around Mrs. McArthur's shoulders as a stole. I was transfixed. She was a smoker, and in a dramatic motion of her lacquered red nails, she used her thumb and fourth finger to grasp a tobacco bit from her tongue, which had been deposited by her unfiltered cigarette. There were no smokers in our household, so I was fascinated. For years after, I would imitate this curious gesture.

Later, when I was eight or nine and my grandparents had retired to San Antonio, my grandmother shocked me by asking me to sit on her lap for the first time. Such a request was foreign to me. I had become as emotionally frigid as she. I did as she asked, but it felt wooden. I was uncomfortable doing so, and I quickly stood and walked away. She never asked again.

Afterword

In my thirties, with the help of newfound faith, I came to see that my grandparents were so broken by the horrific death of their daughter (my mother) that they became frigid toward one another and toward me. They had lost all hope and were left with only the stark reality of their loss. I have forgiven my grandparents for their coldness and deceit and have put away my anger. Forgiveness has set me free. I am no longer an orphan.

MY LAST SOIREES AS A MUSICIAN

Ken Ashworth

When I returned to college from the navy, I changed my major from music to economics. But I had one last pass at my performing career in music before I left it for good.

While in the navy and our ship was visiting Hong Kong, I had come across a Vienna-made, full-size, bass fiddle in a used-furniture store for twenty-five bucks. Back in California, I built a coffin-shaped plywood case in the woodworking shop on the base to ship it home. When I was discharged, I was ready to use my fiddle to work my way through the University of Texas.

I didn't know I was about to tie in with another newly discharged sailor and musician, Jimmy Gough, a commercial art major. With Gough's combo we could play sophisticated jazz, in tux, for sorority parties, or we could go country and western, in boots and jeans, at fraternity parties or raunchy beer joints. A gig was a gig. We earned more on Friday and Saturday nights with our music than we could make any other way as students at UT.

For the first gig I played with Gough, I arrived at a dingy dance hall just south of the old Montopolis Bridge in Austin. Gough and I still had to size each other up. While I unpacked my bass, I asked him why he was moving the bandstand across the room.

"Last Saturday they had a shoot-out here, and some guy got killed. It's better for us to set up by the windows," he said.

A couple of weeks later, our gig across town ran until midnight. At twelve o'clock, with the dance floor packed, Gough said, "I want you to put your bass over your head and start for the door right through the crowd that's standing there waiting for us to start the next number. Go slow."

"Why?"

"We haven't been paid yet, and I know this owner. He's gonna try to stiff us. I want it to look like we're packin' up to leave. So you head for the door. All these people waiting to dance will see the fun's about to end, and they'll start to leave too. You're gonna help me negotiate a good price for playin' a coupla more hours and get our cash up front, right now. Walk slow so nobody can miss seeing you."

Miss seeing me? With a bull fiddle over my head?

Of the several bad gigs I played with Gough, the worst was in a little town maybe north, maybe west of here. Maybe Brownwood, maybe Brady, or Hunt. Gough took another player, Wayne Wood, with him, and I followed in my Plymouth with my bass. Gough took out his "ax" (his guitar), Wood set up his steel guitar and chair, and I unpacked my bass on a stage big enough for a symphony orchestra. As I looked out over the empty, cavernous gymnasium, I asked, "Where are our melody instruments?" I expected something like a trumpet, clarinet, or sax. Gough was evasive and finally said they must have gotten lost. I said we couldn't play that gig with just the three of us.

Gough nodded. "I'll be right back," he said, and headed for the door.

As the crowd started paying admission and filing in, he showed up with a high school kid and a tenor saxophone. Gough puts together the large sax, about half the size of the kid, and hangs it around his neck. He shows him how to hold it and says, "Kid, you play a single note, you're fired."

"You don't need to worry, Jimmy," I said. "There's no reed on his mouthpiece. Where did you get the sax and find him?"

"Borrowed it from a music store. This here's Skeeter. I sort of kidnapped him outside the music store."

I said that Skeeter was just decoration, and we still didn't have a melody instrument.

"Look," Gough shot back, "the kid cost me ten bucks. We'll just have to sing a lot. After they drink for an hour, everything'll be just fine. This way we can split the kitty three ways. It's a good deal."

It was clear he had never planned to have any melody instruments with us. So, we start playing, and the crowd looks really skeptical, but a few folks start dancing—and fortunately the audience begins to drink—a lot. We're getting by. After a while, an old fellow comes up to the edge of the stage between numbers and shouts, "Hey, buddy, I can't hear your sax player."

Gough doesn't miss a beat. "It's going to be a long night," he tells the guy. "He's savin' hisself."

About an hour later, the old fellow comes back. "I still can't hear your sax man." Gough gives him the same line about the kid saving himself, and the fellow says, "Can he play 'Night Train'? It's my favorite sax piece."

Gough takes off his Stetson and waves it in the air and exclaims, "'Night Train'! Fella, that's his best number."

The people running the bar were happy about their sales and we were cheering them on. Wayne Wood had the habit of humming the melodies of songs and his improvisations loudly as he played them on his steel guitar. Jimmy put the mike closer to him. He coached Skeeter in bumping and swinging his sax to our rhythm like he was having fun. Between Wood humming and Jimmy and me singing and Skeeter getting into the swing of things, it looked like we were going to make it through the gig after all. Jimmy had to keep telling the kid to keep the mouthpiece in his mouth—and to stop chewing gum.

Very late in the evening, the same old fellow is clearly feeling his drinks as he stumbles up to the edge of the stage. "Shay, I'm beginnin' ta think maybe I *can* hear your sax man. But whut I wanna know ish whensh he gonna play 'Night Train'?"

Gough takes off his hat and slaps his thigh with it. "Oh, man! Don't tell me you missed it?"

"Aw, I was jush out for a liddle whahle." He chewed on his mustache a minute and then said, "Kin he play it agin?"

"Sorry, pardner," Gough says. "He's only got one 'Night Train' in him for the night. He's plumb wore out."

Gough cut a deal to get us paid for another two hours and free rooms for the night at the motel up the road. He slipped Skeeter an extra five and sent him home.

My music career ended when I left the state for graduate work, and I sold that fine bass for $200.

SHAPED BY OUR EXPERIENCES

Robbie Ausley

When I was growing up in the '50s in Lubbock, Texas, my parents owned a neighborhood grocery store where many in our family worked. As a teenager, I worked there in the summers and after school, along with an elderly Black man named Horace who had worked for our family for years. Horace and my mother had an ongoing struggle—she insisted that Horace come through the grocery store's front door, along with all the other employees who were white, but he insisted, as a Black man, that he must come through the back door. Several times I witnessed Mother's encounters with Horace when she saw him parking in front of the store and walking down the alley to the back door. She would run and lock the back door so he would be forced to come through the front door with the white employees.

My three older brothers and I also enjoyed those days as we spent time with my elderly grandfather, affectionately called "Papaw," while he spent his later years dawdling at our family store. When Horace was asked by my father to work with Papaw in the daily freshening up and replenishing of the produce, a beautiful, caring friendship developed. My older brothers and I still recall Papaw sitting on a wooden crate on that produce aisle while Horace did most of the work. We listened to their laughter and witnessed their care and love for one another. Skin color did not matter to Papaw or Horace—they were just best friends.

Then one day Papaw suddenly became very ill, dying a few days later. As a teenager, I was absorbed in my own sadness, mourning the sudden loss of my grandfather, never thinking about Horace's sadness and his mourning the sudden loss of his best friend, UNTIL—the day of Papaw's funeral.

I was riding in the front seat of the limousine with my mother in the funeral procession from our house to Asbury Methodist Church when I looked up and saw

Horace about two blocks from the church, standing on the street corner, all dressed up in a suit and tie, with his hat on his chest and tears streaming down his face. Confused, I asked Mother, "Why is Horace standing there—why isn't he at the church?" Mother replied so matter-of-factly, "Robbie, Horace is a Black man. Black men are not allowed to go to white men's funerals or be in a white man's church. That's just how it is." That vision of Horace standing on the street corner, excluded and discriminated against because of his skin color, still pains me and will be etched in my heart forever.

For years, I was perplexed at how my mother could be so persistent that Horace be treated as an equal with respect and dignity in our presence with friends and family, yet not question or challenge institutions and policies that did otherwise.

Over twenty years later in the spring of 1980, I came face-to-face with the possibility of impacting discrimination and unequal education in Austin public schools, but it meant busing my four children across town. I believe my experience with Horace shaped our decision not to move to a different neighborhood and not to send our children to private schools. Instead, Tom and I decided to keep our children in Austin public schools and direct our energies toward making sure schools in East Austin were equal to our schools in West Austin. It was not easy that first year of busing, because many parents, students, and teachers were filled with resentment and hatred, as well as anxiety and uncertainty. However, I immediately became involved in the East Austin schools where our children were bused—Johnston High School and Brooke Elementary.

My involvement in East Austin schools eventually moved beyond school activities because other injustices began to raise their ugly heads in the Brooke low-income, minority neighborhood. As President of Brooke PTA, I soon found myself in the middle of a zoning battle with a developer who wanted to roll back the zoning of vacant property across from Brooke Elementary from residential to industrial so he could build a meat rendering plant across from the school. In addition, directly behind Brooke Elementary in the middle of this same neighborhood was a sandblasting company that had been violating state air and noise regulations for years by blasting outside. These conditions of pollution and noise made it difficult for the children at Brooke Elementary to breathe, as well as to hear, during the school day. I kept asking myself, "Would this developer have attempted to zone property as industrial across from Highland Park Elementary or Anderson High School in our affluent Northwest Austin neighborhood? Would this sandblasting company have been able to get away with this type of air and noise pollution for years in Northwest Hills?" Through a court battle with the developer, we kept the East Austin property zoned residential, and years later, it became a low-income residential neighborhood. In addition, we were successful in getting the doors of the sandblasting company behind Brooke Elementary padlocked, and eventually it was forced to close.

During those years of facing injustices and inequality in East Austin, I once again began having that vision of Horace twenty years earlier, standing on the street corner and being treated as unequal, without respect and dignity, and wondering why my mother did not question or challenge institutions and policies that generated those injustices.

Many years later in 2003 before Mother died at age eighty-five, she surprised me with a bold, unexpected statement in a conversation during my last visit with her, proclaiming, "I think the Methodist Church is going to have a black eye for excluding gays from full participation in the church just like they did in the '50s when they excluded Blacks because of their skin color. I am too old to do anything about it, but remember, you're not." Over the last twenty years since her death, Mother's voice to "do something about it" has sometimes haunted me, but I realize it has also been the inspiration that motivates me to stay involved in the Methodist Church's journey to inclusion and full participation of the LGBTQ+ community.

COME TAKE A PICTURE OF MY RATTLESNAKE

Mary Lea Baker

"Come take a picture of my rattlesnake." That was a common request from ranchers to my newspaper-publisher husband during the years we lived in ranching country in far West Texas. The monster rattlesnakes never failed to live up to their reputations. Sure enough, some were granddaddies of all snakes and were as big around as a man's arm. Their photos often appeared on the front page of the *Fort Stockton Pioneer*, our twice-weekly newspaper.

My husband, Frank, came into newspapering naturally. His dad, George Baker, had owned the paper since before Frank was born, and Frank had worked in various jobs in the back shop since he was a small boy. At that time, in the days before digital newspaper production, the back shop was where the action was. Frank earned his degree in journalism from the University of Texas and was hired to be the editor of the *Llano News* while he was still in school.

We loved Llano, and the people were welcoming and understanding as the young editor took over the reins of the paper. We soon learned that a small-town newspaper is almost a utility, though. Everyone in town took ownership, and no one was afraid to express an opinion.

The job was not to last. Five months after we moved to Llano, Frank was drafted into the US Army, and our next few years were spent at Fort Hood, Fort Benning, and in Germany. That's another story, however, and may appear in a future edition of the journal.

When Frank's service in the army was coming to an end, his dad said he needed an advertising manager at the *Pioneer* in Fort Stockton. Could Frank come and help for a year or so? Forty-seven years later, we finally made the move back to Austin so we could be on hand to see our grandchildren play football and participate in other school activities.

As a young bride in Fort Stockton, I soon found that my life had changed completely. I grew up in Longview, in deep East Texas, and I was accustomed to tall trees, lakes, and lush greenery—especially in the spring and summer.

Soon after we moved to Fort Stockton, our daughter Susan was born. One of the first purchases we made for our brand-new baby was a washer and dryer. I tried hanging our laundry outside in the sun, but soon realized that along with the sun came wind and dirt. The laundry was covered with mud balls and had to be washed again. There were days when we could hardly see across our front lawn through the dust, and we felt as though half of Arizona and New Mexico was blowing down our street! Frank learned to be extra nice to me when the wind was blowing.

Many people have asked how we could live in those harsh West Texas conditions for so long. The truth is that I fell in love—first with the people, who are strong, opinionated, caring, and extremely protective of their country and way of life. I also fell in love, eventually, with the countryside itself. There are few things more beautiful to me now than the big valleys, the shadowed mesas late in the evening, and, of course, the world-class sunsets. It is truly the land of the high sky.

As the wife of the new adman, I was expected to be active in the community and, most of all, to shop at home. I'm sure all of that has changed now, with the advent of online shopping. But at the time, it was very important that we support the newspaper's advertising customers.

Before long our other children arrived: our son, Kelly, and daughter Kathy. As the children became more involved in school, I did, too—PTA, PTSA, Girl Scouts and Boy Scouts, Band Aiders, all the school activities, and later the Memorial Hospital Auxiliary. Our church was also important to us and became a focal point for much of our life.

I didn't work outside the home during this time. My degree was in interior design, through home economics. Most people I encountered in Fort Stockton liked to do their own decorating, and they certainly would never have paid someone to do it for them.

My first experience of actually working at the newspaper came about when my mother-in-law, Emily Baker, who was the *Pioneer*'s lifestyle editor, fell and broke her arm. She asked me to fill in for her while she recuperated, and I didn't have the heart to turn her down. My daily life was consumed by attending and reporting on meetings, writing engagement and wedding stories, penning obituaries, and covering anything else pertaining to the social aspects of the community. Stock shows, awards banquets, parades, and service clubs became part of the routine. Because the restored fort (Fort Stockton's namesake) had been listed on the National Register of Historic Places, we were also involved in the events that took place in that part of town.

I soon found myself wearing many other hats at the newspaper as well—proofreader, accountant, page-layout person, and even kitchen cleaner. (Someone had to do it!) The only jobs I didn't try were selling ads, which I refused to do, and darkroom work, which I wanted to learn, but for which I never had time.

Press days were always hectic, because as hard as we tried to bring everything in by deadline, there was still a great deal to accomplish. We eventually moved into the computer age, but for many years before that, we pasted up the pages manually on giant light tables. Since we didn't have a press in Fort Stockton, the next step would be to drive the pages fifty miles to Pecos, where the paper would be printed at the *Pecos Enterprise* shop. We took turns making the Pecos trip and bringing the bundles of newspapers back for our distribution crew to handle the next morning. We had home delivery, and Frank and I occasionally had to throw the papers ourselves. What was easy for our distribution crew turned into a nightmare for us, because we didn't know the routes.

In the early 1970s, Frank's dad was elected to the Texas Legislature, and we purchased the newspaper from him. By then I had gotten printer's ink in my veins and enjoyed the camaraderie and rhythm of working together with the *Pioneer* team. We had a lot of fun, and each of us had a tale about how long we had to wait for Frank to get his front-page column to us so we could move on with the page layout. He was usually busy with advertising, and since that was what kept the paper in business, it took priority.

Frank assembled a crackerjack staff, each of whom had a desire to put out the best and most accurate newspaper possible. It was a large paper and won many awards, including five Sweepstakes awards from the Texas Press Association for best overall semiweekly in Texas.

Life was not all work. We still get together with some of the staff, and when we do, we talk about the fun we had at our birthday parties (held during afternoon breaks) and the games at our Christmas parties. In the early years, everyone dressed up and came to our home for Christmas. Later, Frank took us out to eat, once to a dinner theater in Odessa and another time to the historic Gage Hotel in Marathon.

Also, what turned out to be our family's vacation was a trip each summer to the Texas Press Association conventions in Austin and other Texas cities. Frank, as his dad had been many years earlier, served as president of the organization.

Looking back, it's easy to forget the hectic days and remember only the joy of seeing one more paper in print and knowing we had turned out the best product we could. I've often thought that the small-town newspaper is where the action is, and we took a lot of pride in putting that action into print every week.

MAKIN'S

Floyd Brandt

The sight of a large fading sign in Giddings, Texas, that covered one side of the Orsag's Furniture store advertising "BULL DURHAM Smoking Tobacco - The Old Reliable" evoked a rush of memories: memories of cowboys, of oilfield roustabouts, and of farmers in Oklahoma and the Texas Panhandle, most carrying a small bag of tobacco with a string and a Bull Durham tag hanging from the shirt pocket—his "cigarette makin's." Rolling a cigarette required using the thumb and the first two fingers of one hand to form a half-round small paper tunnel, then half filling it with tobacco from a Bull Durham sack held in the other hand. Then he grasped the paper tab on the tobacco sack with his teeth to close it before returning it to his shirt pocket. Then he used both hands to roll "the makin's" into a misshaped roll, licked it to seal the roll, and gave each end a slight twist to insure that no tobacco was lost. After placing the roll in his mouth and lighting a match, using the leg of his jeans, a fence post, any rough surface, or his fingernail, the smoker was ready to enjoy his "smoke." This was not a simple operation, particularly on a windy day.

For boys in that Depression era, those were important customs. For a few cents one could buy a bag of Bull Durham in almost any grocery store, feed store, drugstore, or filling station. The problem was that of finding a store willing to sell tobacco to young customers like me and my friends. Thousands of boys got their first real "smokes" from a sack of Bull Durham, after experimenting with smoking corn tassels or grape vine.

Bull Durham had its beginning during the Civil War when soldiers from the North and the South used tobacco as a form of currency to acquire coffee and other goods. Because much of the war was waged in tobacco-growing country, tobacco crops and tobacco sheds were raided for tobacco. While waiting for the surrender to be completed, Yankee and Confederate soldiers raided the farm of John Green in Durham Station, North Carolina. They were so impressed with the milder taste of his tobacco that after returning home, they wrote back to Green requesting more of it. He obliged by mailing them packages of his "bright leaf" tobacco.

With W.T. Blackwell as his new partner, Green formed the Bull Durham Tobacco Company. Blackwell's firm bought the company in 1869 when Green died at the age thirty-seven. John Green had taken the symbol of the bull from Coleman's Original English Mustard, produced in Norwich, England. The bull was a popular trademark but was also the subject of possible copyright and trademark infringement. The company overcame that difficulty.

Bull Durham Tobacco, the first national tobacco brand, was manufactured in Durham, North Carolina; by the beginning of the twentieth century, it was said to be the largest tobacco company in the world according to the aggressive advertising efforts of Blackwell's company. In fact, it was reported that the US Army had purchased the company's entire output of tobacco to include in soldiers' war-time rations. The company's salesmen scoured the country looking for prominent buildings on which to paint Bull Durham advertisements, like the sign on the side of the Orsag's Furniture company in Giddings. The artists who painted the signs were called wall dogs. Many of these signs, now faded and called "ghost signs," were painted on brick walls from 1890 to 1960 and still remain for reasons of nostalgia or simple neglect. Many are carefully protected for historic and aesthetic reasons.

The outfield fences of most minor-league baseball teams were also decorated with advertisements, and most fields had Bull Durham signs measuring about twenty-five feet high by forty feet long. The Bull Durham Tobacco Company offered $50 to any player who hit the Bull Durham sign and a carton of Bull Durham to any player who hit a home run. In 1910, the company paid $4,250 in cash and awarded ten thousand pounds of tobacco. The enclosed area where relief pitchers warmed up during a game was called a "bullpen," so named because of the typical Bull Durham sign near the area.

Perhaps there remained a pinch or foul whiff of Bull Durham in Lucky Strikes after the American Tobacco Company had acquired what remained of The Bull Durham Tobacco Company. After one hundred and twenty years on the market, the little sacks were no longer produced, and in 1989 the company stopped producing Bull Durham. However, there are sites on the internet that still sell a sack of Bull Durham for about $20.

A TODDLER'S INTRODUCTON TO PRIMITIVE CAMPING

Shirley Dean

It was the midst of the Great Depression, but my father managed vacations of camping and fishing inspired by his natural interests, professional training, and economy. Dad was a field biologist who taught high school biology and coached all men's sports for a yearly salary of six hundred dollars. It is surprising that he was able to afford a vacation, but through focused frugality and Mom's cooperation, he could.

When he was single, Dad and his buddies would drive from Bowling Green, Ohio, to a remote area of Ontario, Canada, for a two-week fishing and camping getaway every summer. Their campsite was primitive, with absolutely no improvements whatsoever. After he married Mom, the two of them made the same annual trip—once even including his father-in-law. Then it came time to bravely include their daughter, who was almost three years old. This is what I remember (or was told?) about my first Canadian camping trip.

Dad removed the back seat from his 1920-something Willys and refashioned it to hold all the trip gear. He carefully packed in his 1.5-horsepower outboard motor; tent, stakes, and tools; fishing tackle, and a wooden box filled with peat moss and earthworms (known as fishing worms in our family). He added a kerosene lantern and a Coleman stove; cooking and eating utensils and home-canned food; bedding and a few clothes. And off we went.

Leaving at 2:00 a.m. meant that I slept much of the way, but with daylight I was all eyes and ears—until I got car sick, that is. Mom had the same problem; she said it was her big tummy that upset her. (My brother was born the following November.) Dad stopped the car and let us out to walk along the side of the road to breathe fresh air and settle our tummies while he eased the car along behind us.

On arriving at our campsite, Dad hacked away the brush and cleared a space to set up the tent. He built a shelf between two trees and then Mom unpacked and set up her "kitchen" on that shelf. We were settled in. In those wonderful days long ago (the early 1930s), the lake water was unpolluted and safe enough to use for drinking and cooking. Oh, and one more necessity! There being no outhouse at the campsite, Mom gently explained how I was to use the trench Dad had dug. She also made it very clear that this procedure was appropriate only for camping and not for our yard at home.

The memories from that first trip are treasured vignettes. There was a rowboat, probably rented where Dad had bought a fishing license and arranged for a campsite. Once we were settled, the next thing was to take a boat ride. In retrospect, I suspect the ride was not only to please Mom and me, but also to scout for good fishing spots. I remember the funny looking (and strange smelling) life jackets we had to wear. I sat in the bow of the boat, with Mom right behind to watch me and to balance the weight. Then, as now, I loved the fresh, clean smell of the water and the outdoors, and the feeling of wind in my hair.

Dad always chose a lake where the fishing was good; he didn't necessarily look for sandy beaches. So to teach me how to swim, he took the boat out to clear water and in we went. Reportedly, my only comment was "pretty deep, pretty deep." But it worked; that is where and when I both learned to swim and to feel confident even though my feet did not touch bottom. I thoroughly enjoyed being in the water.

I remember meals vividly—lots of fish for supper, which was fine. Mom rolled the filets in cornmeal and fried the best fish ever. But breakfast was always oatmeal with canned milk, served on pie tins that functioned as both bowl and plate. It tasted terrible, but I would never have dared refuse to eat it! I detest the taste of canned milk to this day; I eat my oatmeal with raisins, nuts, brown sugar or maple syrup, and NO milk.

One day Dad scooped up a little minnow from a quiet pool along the shore. I put my minnow in some water in an empty one-pound tin coffee can. (Remember those?) I kept the water fresh and enjoyed his company for a few hours and then left him by the shore when we went for a hike in the woods. We looked for blueberries, wild mushrooms (Dad knew which were edible), and anything else we could hunt and gather. Dad knew the names of all the trees and flowers. He told me then, and repeatedly throughout my childhood, that when we know the names of the plants, birds, and animals around us, we have made friends for life.

When we came back to the campsite several hours later, the can and water were still there, but my minnow was gone. Dad said a gull had probably spotted him and grabbed him for a snack. I cried, of course. Obviously, birds were not immediately my friends on that first camping trip. One had eaten my pet minnow, and the mournful cry of the loons made me sad. "Why are they crying, Daddy?" And some of the strange nighttime noises made me shiver with fear. While trying to fall asleep I heard something like a horse whinny. But there were no horses on our little island. Now that was pretty spooky. I cried, afraid of whatever, but Dad told me it was just a little screech owl.

He showed me a picture of the screech owl in his *Peterson Field Guide to Birds,* and the little fellow looked like a kitten to me. Then I learned to listen for him to tell him goodnight. And while listening, I often heard a great horned owl hooting. In his picture he looked very big and strong; I believed Dad when he told me Mr. Great Horned Owl was keeping a lookout and telling us all is well. Thus began a lifelong friendship with birds.

I had my third birthday during the trip. Mom and Dad provided a store-bought angel food cake, the traditional birthday cake in our family to this day. They used three little dry twigs to light as candles, and sang a rousing "Happy Birthday, Shirley" to me. The gift? I don't remember if there even was one; it didn't matter.

One more thing I do remember quite vividly is the first fish I caught. This *was* a fishing trip after all. After a morning of fishing, Dad let me hold a rod with the line dragging in the water as the little outboard motor chug-chugged us back to camp. Upon arrival Dad reeled in my line and "Surprise, Surprise!" We all celebrated the huge northern pike on my hook— the largest catch of the day— snagged by a gill.

And so began a summer ritual: primitive camping, on an island when possible, leaving no evidence of our presence except a tent footprint and path to the shore that soon would be erased by new growth. The annual camping trips were eagerly anticipated, thoroughly enjoyed, sweetly remembered, and lasted until we moved to North Carolina when I was fifteen. Only twice was the trip not to Canada —one to northern Michigan when we rode the ferry to Mackinac Island, and one to

South Bass Island in Lake Erie. But those are stories for another time. Thanks, Dad and Mom, for the wonder-filled experiences and the treasured memories.

EDUCATION IN THE ERA OF COVID-19

Mary Kevorkian

I have been a member of Delta Kappa Gamma (DKG) for sixty-two years. I was president of the Alpha Chapter from 2020 to 2022. My entire biennium was during the pandemic. Because of this, we held all of our meetings on Zoom, and I worked with my executive board to find interesting programs using that medium.

In early 2020 Laura Ewing and Rosemary Morrow, two members of the Alpha Chapter of Texas State Organization (TSO) of DKG were discussing the need for new ideas for the chapter. One possibility might be to organize and implement a training program for students or teachers. Morrow is a retired faculty member of UTeach, the University of Texas UTeach-Liberal Arts program, which is a professional teacher preparation program for UT Austin undergraduates and post-baccalaureate students who are planning to teach high school English, languages other than English, or social studies. The students participate in field experiences in local area schools that provide an excellent glimpse into the world of teaching. Ultimately, Ewing and Morrow decided that contacting UTeach would be an important first step in developing new materials for the Alpha Chapter.

Ironically, the meeting with UTeach was held at the very time when all schools were about to be closed because of COVID-19. However, professors from UTeach and four Alpha Chapter members began to work together via Zoom to plan and organize training for preservice students. The UTeach faculty suggested the topic of working with multilingual learners, noting that school districts are experiencing an ever-increasing number of English-language learners. Teachers, especially new teachers, must be prepared to meet this need.

The TSO of DKG International has formed a nonprofit foundation, Alpha State Texas Educational Foundation (ASTEF). Its mission statement reads: "The purpose of ASTEF is to provide funding for activities that support professional and personal growth of women educators in Texas and promote educational excellence for Texas students." The Alpha Chapter received ASTEF grants in two successive years, 2020 and 2021. It was exciting to receive these grants. The second one was a new grant created to celebrate the tenth anniversary of ASTEF, so we were the first recipients.

The original idea was to provide a training session on the UT campus. However, in 2020 and 2021, the pandemic required that some adjustments be made. All planning and facilitating were done on Zoom. In addition to planning meetings, a DKG member of Alpha, Dr. Karen Duke, was the liaison and met frequently with a UTeach faculty member to facilitate communication. Duke and Morrow are good friends and respected educators who are involved in DKG at both the state and the national levels. All members of the planning committee were active members of the chapter and either current or former officers of the executive board.

In 2020 the workshop was held on two Saturday mornings. In 2021 it was on one Saturday. Both were broadcast on Zoom.

The goal was to provide staff development training, concentrating on strategies and methods for teaching content and concepts to students who either are not English speakers at all or have limited proficiency in the language.

Chapter members contributed funds for gift cards, which were very popular and greatly appreciated. Members also wrote notes of encouragement and personal experience that were emailed to participants. Members who were part of the planning team attended all the sessions. Because it was important to keep members informed and part of the team, plans and content were presented at chapter meetings. After the workshop sessions, UTeach faculty and the trainers attended the Zoom chapter meetings to provide follow-up and evaluation.

Sixteen of twenty-three students, from a variety of backgrounds, participated. For some, English was not their first language. Their comments in the evaluation were positive. They mentioned the good use of breakout rooms and activities. One noted that the workshop was practical rather than theoretical. Another student said that demonstrations and discussions of strategies that would benefit all kinds of students were the most valuable aspects of the training.

Many of the participants expressed their appreciation for the experience. "Thank you so much for supporting the UTeach program. Before this training, I felt very underqualified in terms of practical teaching skills. After this training, I feel more confident to teach and will be implementing a lot of what I learned immediately with my private Korean tutoring students learning English! Thank you again."

"Thank you so much for all your support! Knowing there are people out there willing to help us and root for us makes us feel valued, appreciated, and supported. Thank you!"

Several aspects of this project contributed to its success. Laura Ewing, a member of the Alpha Chapter, wrote the two successful grant applications. We had a very good working relationship with the UTeach staff and faculty. Through frequent communication with chapter members by email and monthly updates at chapter meetings, I kept them involved. We thought the project was a good opportunity to introduce future educators to DKG.

As a member of the planning committee, I attended all the sessions and really enjoyed meeting the students. They seemed very engaged and interested. In the breakout room sessions I liked talking with them, observing their reactions, and hearing their thoughts about the workshop.

This was a learning experience for me as well. Because of the limitations imposed by the pandemic, I learned to use Zoom and found it to be quite an effective teaching tool. I was soon happily encouraging people to "Zoom in."

Our chapter was especially excited to develop this project with UTeach at UT Austin, because in 1929 UT Austin was where Delta Kappa Gamma was founded, by Dr. Annie Webb Blanton from UT and eleven other educators from throughout Texas.

This article has been adapted from the previously published article cited below and is reprinted here with the permission of the Delta Kappa Gamma Society International.*
Kevorkian, M. (2022). "Collaborative Program between Chapter and Local University: Training in Working with Multilingual Learners." *The Delta Kappa Gamma Bulletin* 89, 2: 34-35.

Mary Kevorkian is the immediate past president of the Alpha Chapter of Delta Kappa Gamma.

*The Delta Kappa Gamma Society International is a professional honorary society of women educators with more than 54,000 members in approximately 2,000 chapters in seventeen countries worldwide. The DKG Society promotes professional and personal growth of women educators and excellence in education.

A LOOK BACK: GROWING UP ALONG THE OHIO RIVER

Ruth Lehman

Humans have always gravitated toward rivers. A river contributes to our success, giving us a reliable source of water for drinking, for fishing, and for agriculture, and sustaining us as a society. Some of the most powerful ancient civilizations grew up along rivers: the Tigris and the Euphrates Rivers in Mesopotamia (8000–2000 BCE), the Yangtze and the Yellow Rivers in China (4000–2000 BCE), the Indus River flowing through Tibet and Pakistan (3300–1300 BCE), and the Nile River in Egypt (3150–30 BCE). Beyond the access to clean water, floodplains along these rivers offered other benefits that attracted people, among them irrigation, hygiene, and ease of transportation, as well as frequent restoration of their fertile soils through flooding.

Floodplains allowed for the development of cities. As societies grew, their ability to control flooding led to larger harvests, better sanitation practices, and easier travel and shipping. They built dams on rivers to provide a range of economic, environmental, and social benefits, including recreation, flood control, water supply, hydroelectric power, waste management, river navigation, and wildlife habitat.

As a child I lived with my parents in several villages along the beautiful Ohio River, and it was there that I began a lifelong love affair with rivers. I've spent a lot of time watching the Ohio and wondering why it affected me so deeply.

In his *Notes on the State of Virginia* (1781–82), Thomas Jefferson stated, "The Ohio is the most beautiful river on earth. Its current gentle, waters clear, and bosom smooth and unbroken by rocks and rapids."

Beginning at Pittsburgh, Pennsylvania, the Ohio River is formed by the confluence of the Allegheny and the Monongahela Rivers. The river ends 981 miles later at Cairo, Illinois, where it empties into the Mississippi.

The name "Ohio" comes from the Seneca, one of the Six Nations of the Iroquois Indian League: Ohi-yo' (Good River). In the late eighteenth century, the Ohio River was the southern boundary of the Northwest Territory. It became a primary transportation route for pioneers, including my ancestors, during the westward expansion of the early United States.

William Henry Nease, Mom's great-great-grandfather, emigrated to the United States from the Rhine Valley in 1765 because of civil unrest, lack of employment opportunities, and political difficulties at home. He settled in Georgetown, Pennsylvania. His son, Henry, went first to the Shenandoah Valley in Virginia, where he married Mary Zirkel, and in 1797, the couple came to the Ohio Valley.

Others joined Henry after hearing his descriptions of the rich Ohio River bottomland that he found there. (Bottomland is flat land a few feet above normal high water, consisting of alluvial deposits. As a result, it is naturally fertile, with less need for fertilizer than land farther up the riverbank.) Henry and Mary had ten children. The Ohio Valley and its river were vital to their success.

In the mid-1930s, during the depths of the Great Depression, my parents were renting some of this bottomland in Letart Falls, Meigs County, Ohio. They used the river to supply income from both fishing and farming. They also utilized it for transportation and as a source of water for washing and cleaning. And a power station on the Ohio was the source of their electricity.

On the other hand, their drinking water came from a cistern (a waterproof tank that Dad built for catching and storing rainwater). The Ohio River was, and still is, one of the most polluted rivers in the United States, according to the U.S. Environmental Protection Agency. Its banks are highly populated and industrialized, and for generations it served as a dumping ground for local cities and industries.

Mom and Dad were truck farming the rich bottomland. Historically, the term "truck farming" had nothing to do with trucks. It meant the cultivating of vegetables for marketing. Truck farming began after the Civil War as cities grew and the arrival of railroads made transporting produce faster and more efficient. Among the most prevalent truck crops were strawberries, tomatoes, melons, turnips, cabbages, and potatoes.

Because keeping good records was important in evaluating which crops succeeded and which did not, Mom kept a daybook in which she recorded their truck-farming data. Extracts from her *Daybook I*:

Aug. 3. 1936: Worked in strawberries.

4: Picked tomatoes and hoed strawberries.

5: Plowed and hoed strawberries

6: Picked and packed tomatoes. Rained out at noon. Best rain we've had for weeks.

7: Too wet to work in the ground. Ralph picked melons [cantaloupes].

8: Pulled weeds out of strawberries.

9: Sunday. Picked tomatoes and melons in morning.

10: Picked tomatoes and cantaloupes.

12: Picked tomatoes and cantaloupes.

14: Picked tomatoes and cantaloupes; hoed strawberries in afternoon.

16: Sunday. Rained in morning; picked cantaloupes.

17: Picked toms [tomatoes] and cantaloupes.

Sept. 14: Canned beans. Ralph put up soybeans.

16: Ralph plowed the strawberry ground today.

17: Ralph plowed potato and tomato ground.

18: Ralph gathered 18 bu. of turnips, 9 of which he put in the cellar.

28: Finished making ketchup. Have 46 pints.

Oct. 27: Ralph pulled tomato stakes.

28: First frost last night.

Nov. 26: Ralph hauled straw for our strawberries.

27: Ralph strawed the berries.

28: Ralph hauled dirt for his cabbage bed, and scattered straw on the strawberries.

30: Ralph helped haul 28 bbl. [barrels] water for the cabbage house, repaired tomato bed in afternoon.

Several times Mom's daybook mentions that they "hoed strawberries." They cultivated around the base of each plant (strawberry, tomato, melon, etc.) with a hoe, working the soil only deep enough to kill the weeds, being careful not to damage the plant's root system.

Some of the common weeds had delightful and/or fascinating names: Queen Anne's lace, oxeye daisy, sensitive fern, dandelion, staghorn sumac, crown vetch, shepherd's purse, creeping Charlie, joe-pye weed, bouncing bet, touch-me-not, coltsfoot, smartweed, mouse-ear chickweed, nodding beggarticks, pigweed, sowthistle, dodder, bitter sneezeweed, water knotweed, pokeweed, horse nettle, deadnettle, and burdock.

Living within the Ohio River floodplain, we experienced a number of floods, including the disastrous 1937 flood. In that flood 385 people died, one million people were left homeless, and property losses reached $20 million, according to the National Oceanic Atmospheric Administration's National Centers for Environmental Information.

During the 1937 flood, we were living in a two-story brick house, the oldest house in Letart Falls, probably more than one hundred years old. The town of Letart Falls, established in 1797, was one of the first settlements in Meigs County. The Ohio River forms the eastern and part of the southern boundary of the county, where it appears to outline the shape of an elegant high-heeled boot. We were living six miles upriver from Racine in the "toe" of the "boot."

This old house, known as the Caldwell House but often referred to as "the Brick," was partitioned and rented as a two-family house. We lived on the second floor, which had an exterior stair. The house had electricity, but no plumbing or heating. Our coal-burning kitchen stove supplied heat for the second floor, and as mentioned, a cistern normally supplied our drinking water.

The house, located on the riverbank, had withstood quite a number of floods, including the 1913 flood, which some sources still consider the greatest natural disaster in Ohio history. Property damage from that flood was estimated to be more than $100 million, and 467 Ohioans lost their lives.

January 1937 was unusually warm, and the melting of the snow cover, the thawing of the ice along the edges of the river, and fourteen days of rain had caused the waters to rise to their highest levels in recorded history. Rain began falling on the evening of January 9 and continued with only brief interludes until January 23. Combined with runoff from melting snow in the nearby hills, the rains pushed the river well above flood stage, ultimately to a record 51.1 feet. Communities like ours throughout the Ohio Valley suffered heavy damage.

Extracts from Mom's *Daybook I*:

Jan. 7 [1937]: Very warm ever since Christmas. Girls and boys playing outdoors this evening without even sweaters on.
9: Warm, dark, misty day. Drizzled toward evening.
10: Rained hard all night.
11: [The Ohio] River surely jumped up the bank last night. Ralph had to move fodder on top of the bank.
14: Warm and rainy. Ralph helped Bert butcher.
15: Rained all last night.
17: Rained all last night and all day today. River is over the road at Harry Manuel's.
18: Rained hard all last night. No school today because of water over the road.
20: Was cooler last night, and we thought we could butcher today, but this morning it was warm and raining. That hog has had more reprieves than Bruno Hauptmann! River is still raising.
Rained nearly all night and drizzled till noon. Franklin D. Roosevelt took oath of office for second term today.
21: Rained all last night and all day today.
22: Rained all last night and all day today. River broke over the bank this morning. Everyone moving out in the lower part of Letart [Falls]. Ralph took "the hog with the charmed life" up to Chapman's this morning, and we took the canned goods and kindling out of the basement. River is higher tonight than it ever was last spring. [Our] Skiff [a flat-bottom boat with a pointed bow and a square stern, making it especially maneuverable in shallow water] tied to the electric-light pole in front of the house tonight.
24: Moved furniture upstairs. Water came all around the house and filled cellars. Everyone on lower side of street moving furniture out of upstairs windows. Electric went off this afternoon. Moved our things

into one room, and Sarsons [family living on ground floor] moved their things upstairs. We left Brick after dark and went out to Pickens'. Warm and rainy.

25: River still raising. Folks moving every way you look. Went over to Brick about 4:00. River was over the front porch but not in the house yet. The Brick was last house to get floor wet on that street. Everyone moving night and day. Gasoline for trucks getting scarce. Colder in afternoon. Rowed skiff in about 12 ft. of water over our cabbage patch, where we cut cabbage last summer no bigger than a coffee cup due to the drought.

26: Lucy, Elva, Flossie [Pickens], the children, and I went up to [Will] Crow's store. When we went up the road was dry, but we walked through water coming back between Bart Miller's house and the store. Cold today.

27: River raised only about 2 in. last night. On a stand today [no longer rising]. Sam Mors was drownded last night getting feed out of Beegle's. store at Racine [one of 385 people who lost their lives].

28: Cloudy, misting. River fell 9 in. last night.

29: Water went out of Brick last night. WPAs [Works Progress Administration] are sweeping out houses. [A thick coat of smelly mud covered everything.] Went in a boat with Ralph to the Brick and got a few dirty clothes to wash.

30: Sarsons took their things back downstairs. Ralph set our range [coal-fired kitchen stove] up upstairs, and we came back to the Brick about 4:00. A real spring day. Flowers are up in the mud around the house. Small buildings, garages, coal houses lying all over Bucktown [an area of Letart Falls]. Got a box of clothing for children and food supplies from flood relief.

31: The last day of January. A very warm month, dark, a world of rain, not a day cold enough to butcher. The hog with the charmed life still alive. The biggest flood since 1913 [62.2 at Cincinnati: Cincinnati Weather Bureau]. Lacked 17 inches of equaling the 1913 flood [80.0: Cincinnati Weather Bureau] here. River dropped back under the bank last night. Dropped very fast after it started. Old Mrs. Smith, 93 years old and watched the river all her married life, said you never need to move drift [floating debris] from a flood in Jan. as the river would take the drift away before planting time. This afternoon nearly everyone in Letart [Falls] is down looking over Bucktown.

Feb. 1: The river was down in its banks and several towboats going up [the river] this afternoon. Everyone down here scratching around in the mud, fixing up houses and outbuildings.

2: Raining again this morning when we got up. Ralph helped Elza [Birch, who lived across the street] fix his furnace. I scrubbed the downstairs.

3: WPA men cleaning out cisterns. Ralph went to Middleport and helped Clarence C[hapman] move furniture downstairs in his store.

6: Very cold this morning. Ralph butchered the hog this morning.

7: Sunday. Dark, cold. Drizzled occasionally all day.

8: Had a real thunderstorm last night and the hardest downpour of rain I have heard since I have been in this house. Rained for about 5 hours. River is ugly, muddy-looking, and raising 6 in. per hour. Day was windy as March, hot—64° at Athens. I rendered the lard this afternoon. [Rendering is the process of melting pork fat and straining it to remove meat scraps, veins, and impurities.]

9: Rained all last night and most all morning. Cooler this evening. I fried down sausage this afternoon. [After the choice cuts—i.e., hams, tenderloins, chops, and bacon—were removed, the rest of the meat was cut out and ground into sausage, which was then seasoned with spices and shaped into patties or stuffed into a gut to make sausage links.]

12: Bright, spring-like day, not very cold. Ralph worked at rebuilding tomato cold frames [a bottomless box with a transparent roof that is set over a plant to protect it from the cold].

13: Bright sunny morning, overcast in afternoon, uncomfortably warm in evening. Ralph worked at cold frames. Turned the cow dry. [The udder of a dairy cow requires a non-lactating rest-period prior to her upcoming calving in order to optimize milk production in the subsequent lactation needed for the calf.]

14: Sunday. Very high wind blowing all day. Dark with occasional snow flurries, a weird, ugly day. The wind moans around the corners of this old house tonight, rattles the roof and bangs the screen doors. And Sarsons' 3 dogs BARK. Ralph and I have been married 7 years today. There are no plum trees around here. [!!]

15: Snowed most of the morning, but melted off quickly this afternoon.

16: Rained all last night, turning to snow about daylight. Snowed till about noon, most all melted off this afternoon.

21: Sunday. Sunshine, rain, hail, sleet, high winds and thunder: "something different every minute," the [Athens, Ohio] Messenger says.

23: A surprise visit from Winter. A beautiful snow on this morning, all the branches covered with snow, and snowing big, soft flakes. Was most all melted off by noon.

24: Bright and rather cold. Ralph sowed the tomato seed today [in the cold frames].

26: This about the coldest day this winter.

28: Sunday. Sunshine and cold. Today finished up February. Nine snows this month, but all melted almost as fast as they fell.

Being privileged to live on the Ohio River's banks, I often sat just watching the water, focusing my attention on its speed and sound. I could look at it almost indefinitely because its beauty never wearied me. It changed from hour to hour.

The migratory and backyard birds and woodland wildlife I saw while watching the river needed reliable water sources, too. Every living thing on earth needs water to survive. It's an amazing fact that the water we drink today is the same water that dinosaurs, woolly mammoths, and the first humans drank! Earth has only a certain amount of water, and it travels around, moving between lakes, rivers, oceans, the atmosphere, and the land. The only thing that changes is the form that water assumes as it travels through the cycle.

Since ancient times, we humans have assigned healing and transformational properties to water. In Chinese medicine and traditional Indian medical wisdom, water was crucial to balancing the body and creating physical harmony. In early

Rome, baths were an important part of social life, a place where citizens went to find relaxation and to associate with others in a calming setting.

Rivers have long been seen as sacred places, and in a number of transcendental contexts, water has symbolized rebirth, spiritual cleansing, and salvation. So it's not surprising, given that for many thousands of years humans have needed water to survive, that it's in our nature to seek out large expanses of water.

Fairly recent studies have suggested that our brains are hardwired to react positively to water. Being near, in, or on water makes us happier, healthier, and more relaxed, both mentally and physically. The sound of rippling water is far simpler than the sound of voices, the sound of music, or the sound of a city. Rivers can give our brains and our senses a rest from overstimulation.

Everyday life can be rife with stressful moments: a delayed flight, the pressure of upcoming bills, a setback at work, overwhelming family responsibilities, or a dispute with a loved one. Different circumstances can leave anyone feeling wrung out for different reasons. And all of this is piled on top of already stressful conditions, where one's mind is never at rest, always moving from one obligation to the next and from one thought to another.

Learning how to calm down and compose ourselves can help us manage those stressful moments and take care of our minds and our bodies. To that end, the beautiful Ohio River still endures in my loving memories of it, but it also raises the larger questions of why rivers are important to humans, why it is in our nature to want to be near them, and what we can do now to preserve these essential ecosystems.

AN AFRICAN MERCHANT OF VENICE

Ben Lindfors

"You interested in dramatics?"

"In watching plays, yes. But I've never acted in one."

"Could you direct a school play?"

"I suppose I could try."

"Jolly good," the headmaster said. Quickly, before I could object, he seized the Extra Duties Roster and wrote my name down as "Master in Charge of Dramatics."

I left the headmaster's office wondering what I was in for. As well as knowing nothing about acting or directing, I had never worked with African students before. It was my second day at Kisii Secondary School, an African boys' boarding school in western Kenya. The students, 240 strong, would be coming back from their holidays in one short week to begin a new term.

I tried to remember what had been said during my orientation course in New York in the summer of 1961 about secondary school students in Kenya. One fact stuck in my mind: in Kenya only one boy in a hundred gets a secondary school education. The students are weeded out by competitive examinations. Therefore, the students I would be working with were the cream of the crop, the top one percent in the whole country. This statistic was comforting to me as a teacher but disconcerting to me as the new "Master in Charge of Dramatics." I wondered how much more they knew about dramatics than I did. How many plays had they read? How many had they seen performed? How many had they performed themselves?

When I asked the headmaster these questions the next day, he only shrugged his shoulders and said that in the four months he had been in Kisii, there had been no plays performed at the school. "About time we rejuvenated the dramatics club, isn't it?" he concluded.

Still eager to get answers to my questions, I sought out two teachers who I knew had been at Kisii more than four months. Both said they had never seen the students put on a play. One teacher had been at Kisii for two years.

I thought back on the headmaster's words. "Rejuvenated," indeed! The dramatics club would have to be resurrected from the dead.

A week later I had the opportunity to put my questions to the students themselves. I decided to ask the Form Four (Senior class) boys first, since they had been in school the longest.

"What plays have you read in school?

"ˆ*Merchant of Venice*, sir."

"Yes, of course. We are starting to read that now. But what other plays have you read at school?"

"None, sir."

"None, are you quite sure?"

Heads nod.

"Well, what plays have you read outside of school?"

Silence.

"Has anyone ever seen a play performed?"

Several affirmative responses.

"When?"

"When we were in Form One, sir. A church in town had a Christmas play. Some of us saw that one."

"Well, it's about time we started a dramatics club, isn't it?"

Thus, by bringing together actors who did not know how to act and a director who did not know how to direct, the Kisii School Dramatics Club was born.

Disappointed at first by my students' naïveté, I was cheered during the next few weeks by their classroom behavior. I found they were wonderfully expressive. When a boy couldn't find the right English words to answer a question, he would get his idea across with animated gestures. When reading aloud, they tried to read with expression. Unlike many American students, they showed no reluctance to speak or perform before their classmates. Their delightfully uninhibited acting gave me hope; this, I said to myself, is the stuff that good plays are made of.

One day I took my Form Four students up to the dining hall for a literature class. A small stage had been constructed at one end of the hall, and I wanted to see how the students would handle themselves on it. It was here that my rising expectations suffered a tragic fall. Put on stage with memorized speeches cluttering their brains, these same students who had always spoken and moved with such remarkable vitality were suddenly transformed into armless, legless, tongueless robots. Some of them didn't even blink their eyes through thirty lines of iambic pentameter. After fifteen minutes I feared I was becoming hypnotized, so I stopped the parade of tin soldiers and we played charades for the remainder of the class period. As I watched them return to their normal ebullient selves, I realized that getting them to act naturally while mouthing memorized words was going to be a major task.

Fortunately, selecting a play was not difficult. Since the play was to be virtually the first experience of stage acting for both the actors and the audience, it was important to choose a play that everyone in the school knew. The *Merchant of Venice* was the logical choice since all the Form Four students were studying it at the time and the remainder of the students were familiar with the story through *Tales from Shakespeare*, a required text for Form One (Freshman) English.

I set to work simplifying the language of the play so that the younger students would have no trouble understanding it. Later, after the first tryouts for the play, I found that there was no one suitable to play Launcelot Gobbo, Jessica, or Lorenzo, so I cut out the subplot involving them and took several other measures to simplify the action in the play. I continued to chop and slice at the script until I was satisfied that, with one intermission and a short "dumb show" (pantomime) to introduce the play, the entire performance would last about one hour and a half.

Selecting a cast presented some problems. First, there was a problem of abundance. Though none of the boys knew anything about dramatics, nearly all of them wanted to take part in the play. When fifty-eight out of sixty boys in Form Four signed up for tryouts, I decided to make the *Merchant of Venice* a Form Four production exclusively. This partly solved the problem; there were still too many would-be actors, but at least the abundance was restricted to only one class in the school. I would not have to watch 230 boys try out for the three principal leads.

Ironically, when tryouts began, I discovered that a greater problem than abundance was scarcity. There were plenty of boys who wanted to act, but very few who could act at all. Most of them still suffered from acute stage paralysis and lockjaw. The Shylocks who weren't petrified into granite-like immobility were a forest of wooden gestures. Selecting boys for roles became a matter of trying to decide whether a stick or a stone best represented flesh and blood. When I stopped looking for signs of talent and tried, on the basis of voice, physique, and personality, to find boys who most resembled the characters in the play, selecting a cast became an easier job. Immediately I discovered a spritely Gratiano, a princely Morocco, an arrogant Aragon. Several qualified for Bassanio and Antonio, and one, if he could be made to appear more hard-hearted, would make an admirable Shylock.

But what could be done about Portia and her waiting lady, Nerissa? There was no girls' school to draw upon, so two boys would have to be selected to these roles. Portia would have to be shorter than Bassanio, and Nerissa, compared to a "small, scrubbed boy" in the play, would have to be one of the smallest boys in the class. Neither Portia nor Nerissa could have a bass voice and would have to appear as ladylike as possible. Above all, the boys chosen for Portia and Nerissa would have to be intelligent and mature young men who could cope not only with their parts but also with the comments of their classmates. Boys acting in roles meant for girls might become special objects of ridicule. I had to find two boys who could endure or ignore or, better yet, stifle such ridicule. The boy finally selected for Portia was the top student in his class; although lacking some of Portia's dynamic qualities, he commanded everyone's respect and could deliver difficult lines with ease and grace. Nerissa was a boy who had been eliminated earlier from men's parts because of his high-pitched, scratchy voice; he approached his role with such eagerness, energy, and obvious delight that soon he became more envied than ridiculed.

Minor roles were not difficult to fill. When one boy refused to take the part of Tubal, Shylock's friend, because he didn't "admire" him, five of Tubal's admirers stepped forward to offer their services. I had planned to give walk-on parts to some of the better-oiled robots, but tryouts produced such a surplus of efficient automatons that I inserted several more supernumerary messengers, guards, and servants into the play.

Mimeographed copies of the pruned and grafted script were distributed at the first meeting of the full cast. It was read aloud at that time and was read and walked through at the second meeting. The boys were told to learn their parts during the coming school vacation so that at the first meeting four weeks later, they would be able to go through the entire play without scripts.

During the vacation I organized a schedule of rehearsals and tried to figure out how to stage the play without spending money. Since there was no allowance in the school budget for dramatics, the play would have to be produced on a shoestring. "We can scrape together fifty shillings (about seven dollars) from emergency funds," the headmaster said, "but sorry, no more than that." Seven dollars would have to provide four stage sets and twenty-three costumes. For the stage sets, simplicity was the answer. "Venice, a street" became a bare stage with unpainted plywood sections in the background. "A Court in Venice" became eight classroom chairs, a classroom lectern, and the same plywood sections in the background. "Belmont. Portia's House" became two classroom chairs, a table draped with dormitory curtains, three old boxes painted gold, silver and lead, and the ever-present plywood background. Cost of minute quantities of gold, silver, and lead paint—six shillings. Cost of plywood—thirty shillings.

With only fourteen shillings (two dollars) left to clothe twenty-three actors, I started to seriously consider paper costumes, school uniforms, modern dress, tribal dress—anything in fact short of complete nakedness. I was spared the agony of deciding whether to put the cast into crepe paper, khaki shorts, or monkey skins by the generosity of a secondary school 300 miles away in Uganda. This school had just finished a production of *Merchant of Venice* and agreed to let us borrow their splendid satin costumes. Joyfully, I swore to the director of their dramatics club that I would forfeit a pound of my flesh if the costumes were not returned promptly.

The boys in the cast came back to school full of enthusiasm, but certain key players—Bassanio, the Prince of Morocco, the Duke of Venice—had been unable to perfect their parts because they had spent every day, sunrise to sunset, helping their family bring in the peanut crop. Word came that Portia had not been able to raise enough money to pay all of his tuition, so he wouldn't be returning to school until the third week of the term. I reorganized the schedule of rehearsals, set the tentative performance date later by a few weeks, and hoped there would be no further delays. But more delays there were, some unavoidable, others avoidable. For example, a rehearsal of Act Two might open this way:

Master in Charge of Dramatics (stalks the dining hall, glowers at the assembled cast, and howls):

"Where's Shylock?"

Chorus: "In bed, sir. He's got malaria again."

M.C.D.: "Well, where's the Prince of Aragon?"

Voice (offstage): "He's not here, sir."

M.C.D.: (forte) I KNOW THAT!" (piano) "Where, pray tell, is he?"

Bassanio: "He's captain of the volleyball team, sir. They are practicing for the match on Saturday."

(A cloudburst outside. Tropical rain falling on the tin roof of the dining hall drowns out the words of the M.C.D., but the cast is seen to exeunt quickly as he approaches gesturing violently.)

Rehearsals convinced me that the show would be a flop. It had a chance of partial success as a spectacle because the costumes were dazzling. But I was sure that the awkward mechanical movements would make the actors unrecognizable as human beings, and the mumbled speeches, missed cues, and timing errors would make the spectacle incomprehensible as a story.

I took my seat on the night of the performance weary from many unsuccessful wars against sticks and stones and robots. Crowded into the hall were five hundred students, townspeople, peasant farmers, and children, most of them about to watch their first live dramatic performance. I wondered how many would be disappointed by our comedy of errors, how many would scratch their heads and conclude that stage plays were much ado about nothing.

The hall hushed into complete silence as the footlights flickered on. After a pause and some very audible backstage whispers, the curtain divided, a tree named Bassanio confronted a tree named Antonio, their limbs met and their jaws creaked. These two petrified forest creatures probably would have remained rooted to the spot, but just then there came a sound from the audience, a very audible sigh of satisfaction and appreciation. That sigh, the first involuntary reaction of the audience, transformed Bassanio and Antonio. After several more sounds of approval from the audience, Bassanio and Antonio were completely at ease as human beings. Only a trace of woodenness remained. Still more remarkable, the remainder of the cast underwent the same magical transformation: on first entrance, stiff and unnatural; then after the first sound from the audience, complete relaxation and astonishing histrionic heights. The response of the actors to the reactions of the audience improved the performance tremendously. There were still plenty of imperfections and blunders, but never before had there been such wonderful spontaneity and zest. Unlike the rehearsals, the performance was bursting with life.

The audience loved it. Contrary to expectation, they understood the speeches, followed the action, laughed in all the appropriate places, and applauded wildly at the end. When the entire cast reappeared to bow, the spectators, almost mad with delight, gave them a deafening ovation.

No one clapped longer or louder than I did. If my sides had not been so sore from laughing, I would have joined in the shouting too. Never had I enjoyed a performance more. Congratulating the cast afterward, I told them this was the noblest "Merchant" of them all. When one of the cast asked, "What would Mr. Shakespeare have said about it." I answered with assurance, "No doubt, he would have called it a hit, a very palpable hit."

ONBOARD WITH CATS AND KIDS

Katherine McIntyre

I remember standing by her chair in the living room with Bernie and our kids. I was patting my mother on the head, and we were both crying. We had made a stop to say goodbye to my parents in our hometown in Massachusetts. We had just left Providence, where we had packed all our household goods in a moving van, sold our house, and were starting a big adventure.

We had lived in Providence for four years while Bernie attended graduate school at Brown, our kids had started nursery school and kindergarten, and I had kept house. We had bought a small house in anticipation of staying in the area. Bernie had finished a PhD in theoretical physics and looked forward to getting a teaching job. But the market for newly minted physicists was very slim. His only job offer in response to hundreds of resumes sent to universities and colleges was from a university in Denton, Texas. When you have just one offer, it doesn't take long to make the decision.

It was my mother's birthday, August 15, and we were leaving that day for Texas. I remember thinking that this was a role reversal. My mother should be patting my head, but I was comforting her. We all dried our tears and started for Texas.

It was a crowded car with three young kids, two adults, and two Siamese cats. The cats' only experience being in a car was for a trip to the vet, and they raced around the car from seat to seat until they realized that this car was not going to a vet clinic. Then they decided to sit on top of the front seat—one on the driver side and the other on the passenger side. From that vantage point the cats had a clear view of the scenery as we drove. The kids all sat together in the back seat. We have three sons, and they were good travelers. We carried a load of books and magazines in a gym bag. We had always seat-belted the kids so they stayed put once we started driving.

The car was a little Ford Falcon, the economy model for Ford. Air conditioning is an option in the northeast—nice to have on a hot summer day. As we drove south, we realized that it was less and less an option. Maybe our next car. We rolled the windows part way down, but not too far because we were afraid the cats might get anxious and try to squeeze out the windows. Just far enough down to catch a breeze.

A graduate-school friend had ordered a map book from AAA for us. (Remember them? They were a huge improvement over an atlas.) The small book of folded pages detailed the drive from Providence to Denton. Each page showed routes, landmarks, and a series of yellow marker arrows that kept you moving south. Even a novice driver could follow those pages. We stopped in St. Louis, and everyone enjoyed playing in the zoo. Then we went to the Anheuser- Busch plant, where we saw the Clydesdale horses.

We were budget travelers, camping and making our own meals. The third night out we splurged on a hotel. Bernie took the kids to the pool while I nursed a cracking headache with a nap. We were almost there. On the fourth day of the trip we arrived in Denton and decided to have dinner on the square. Denton is the county seat, and the courthouse dominates the square. It was taller than anything else in the area, and we could see it as we drove in. We had never seen a courthouse like that and thought it must be some kind of church. It is a spectacular building and still dominates the square.

We walked around the square to give our kids a chance to stretch and run off some energy. I remember an abundance of dead crickets in store windows. Getting inside to escape the August heat hadn't saved them. We found a little restaurant and took a break. On his interview trip to Denton in July, Bernie had rented a house for us. Its owner met us at the restaurant and gave us keys to the house. It was a lovely, small structure in an area of Denton that had not yet been built out, so we were surrounded by fields. We found it and ended our trip.

Being part of a university community meant you were going into a setting that welcomed you. Faculty came from all over the country. This was fifty-plus years ago, so faculty meant mainly men—especially in the sciences. We were young, and our kids were just entering the school system. To fund our rather spartan lifestyle of raising kids while going to graduate school, Bernie had a teaching assistant salary, a GI Bill stipend for his years of service in the US Marine Corps, and taught high school math for two hours every morning at a private school. After many years of being on a strict budget, we had an income that is meager by today's standards but was a quantum leap from his income as a graduate student. We were living!

BRAZIL BIRD BRAWL

Tracy Novinger

After three generations of my family had lived on Aruba, an arid island in the Caribbean with an area of only 140 square miles, my father accepted a job with Petrobrás, and my immediate family moved to Brazil. The country spreads out over 3,287,597 square miles; it is larger than the contiguous United States which, excluding Alaska and Hawaii, has an area of 3,119,884 square miles. Our new world was a big change from our previous domain. We were to hear Portuguese instead of Papiamento.

One of the great treats in this huge country, about which we knew so little on arrival, was the abundance and variety of the foods that were available to us there. The staple diet of Brazilians is rice and beans, the rice always well-seasoned with onion, garlic, and tomatoes. There were also many kinds of vegetables, some of which were totally unfamiliar and seemed quite exotic. We lived in the port city of Santos where we could buy delicious fresh seafood daily, as well as meat of excellent quality. The house that my father rented for us to live in had many kinds of trees that grew in the backyard, and the fruits were a special treat. I recall one in particular. The king of the back garden was a majestic avocado tree that towered over everything; it had a huge spread of branches and stood taller than our two-story house. When the avocados were in season, there were more than we could possibly eat. I would pick them with a long bamboo pole that had a small net at one end. Snagging one avocado at a time, I would carefully lower it to the ground so that I would not bruise it. When I had several bags full, my brother and I would distribute avocados to various neighbors on our block. I must say, however, that we kept a huge quantity that we ourselves consumed. We would cut an avocado in half, pry out the large seed, eat the buttery green flesh with a spoon or add it to a salad with a vinaigrette dressing. We also learned to make pale green and sugary avocado "smoothies" as do the Brazilians—but I liked avocados best plain or in a salad.

One very special luxury, however, did not grow on trees—this was the excellent, grass-fed beef that came from the regions south of our city. When I think back to the indulgence of eating a tender, flavorful filet mignon in a sandwich for a simple lunch, my mouth still waters.

In the city of Santos where we lived, customers often ordered their beef from the nearest butcher shop. An Englishwoman living in Santos, who had made little effort to learn any Portuguese, once asked my mother how to ask for soup bones. "I am so tired of going to the butcher shop. I have to pull up my skirt and point at my knee to try to tell that man what I want."

When Brazilians placed their meat orders by phone, they usually requested that it be delivered to their home. Under the hot Brazilian sun, it was common to see a man arrive by bicycle to deliver meat. One delivery stands out in my memory; I was about fourteen years old at the time. As the delivery man pedaled his bike down our street, he held a tray of raw, uncovered meat on his handlebars, skillfully securing the tray with his thumbs. On that particular day, I watched as he arrived at a neighbor's house; the cyclist got off his bike and stood beside it. As was customary, he clapped his hands and waited outside the front yard that had the common chest-high front wall built between the sidewalk and the front garden. The man clapped again and from the house a woman's voice responded to the cyclist's clapping. "I'll be right out," she called through a window protected by iron bars. The front door of the house opened, the woman stepped into the glass enclosure of her covered front patio and proceeded to unlock the patio door that faced the street. When she came to the gate, the delivery man put down the bike's kickstand and left the tray expertly balanced on his bicycle's handlebars. In one upturned bare hand he held the raw meat being delivered up at shoulder height and carried the customer's order to her.

At this point, I became aware of a shadow that began to circle the scene. Apparently, the *urubús (Coragyps atratus)*, the local black vultures, had become well accustomed to the delivery routine, and I suspect that, like me, they also had developed quite a taste for filet mignon.

The cyclist stood with his back to the bike as he handed the meat to the customer. He was waiting to collect payment when the winged thief saw its chance.

The bird's movement must have caught the man's eye because he whirled around just in time to see the opportunistic poacher swoop down and sink its talons into a whole tenderloin that was still sitting on the delivery tray. The *urubú* almost made off successfully with its booty, but the weight of the meat slowed it down. The man was able to run and jump up just in time to get a firm grip on one end of the tenderloin before it could be carried completely out of reach. The vulture flapped its wings and contorted, unwilling to let go of its prize, even though the man yelled and beat at the bird with his free hand. I must say that some of the words he was yelling I had never heard before. Ultimately, the man prevailed in the brawl and successfully wrestled back the contested cut. Thwarted, the bird flew up, circled a few times, and flew off in defeat.

In the end, despite the *urubús'* foray, the contested loin would be delivered to a customer who would eat it. Although subjected to sun, heat, dust, and the talons of a carrion eater, the filet was probably not too much the worse for the wear —at least not visibly.

I sometimes wonder what the meat that I ate in my sandwiches in Brazil might have been through and just where it had been. Is that why those sandwiches tasted so good? They certainly were very flavorful!

THE THIRTY-EIGHTH STREET MEDICAL COMPLEX — HOW IT ALL BEGAN

Theo Painter

In the 1960s, a small group of five or six doctors got to thinking that we could collaborate and build medical offices for our own use. We wanted to be in a central location, have adequate parking, and provide a building with the many specialties of medicine for the convenience of the patient.

We were lucky to get advice from a friend, M. K. Hage, who was known for his expertise in real estate and business. We were also fortunate that the first parcel of land that we looked at was an eleven-acre lot on 38th Street, one of the major streets in central Austin. The lot extended from 34th Street to 38th Street and included an area across Shoal Creek. Around this large lot were numerous small residences on small lots, and we were able to acquire 190 of these. Mr. Hage advised us that doctors go individually to the homeowners to buy their properties. The result was that we owned a large amount of property west of Lamar Boulevard, including what is now Bailey Square, as well as some property in East Austin (the Perry Estate).

We formed a corporation and named it the Austin Doctors Building Corporation. We had sixty-five shareholders, all being doctors or dentists except Mr. Hage and his sister.

I was elected president of the corporation (since no one else would take it). I enjoyed the challenge of the work and spent lots of time with lawyers and bankers especially. I maintained the office for more than ten years. We hired as lawyers Robert Sneed and Sam Perry. The corporation had only two employees, Mr. Hage and his secretary, the latter being our only paid employee. Our architects were Fehr and Granger. We designed a very fine building with wide halls, high ceilings, and 900 total parking spaces, many underground.

As plans developed, it became obvious that a hospital in this area would be a significant and supportable addition. Seton Hospital's facilities were aged by this time, and so after lengthy negotiations, Seton decided to move to our area. We ended up buying fourteen acres of land which we sold to Seton at our cost. In that way, our corporation was instrumental in Seton's relocating, thus changing the face of health care in Austin.

At that time, Congress had voted on a new type of hospital called an "extended care" hospital, and Holiday Inn had been developing these hospitals around the country. We contacted them and they built a 250-bed hospital on the west side of Shoal Creek. The extended care idea was not carried through by Congress, however, and the hospital ended up becoming a psychiatric hospital.

The office building, Medical Park Tower, was so successful that it was fully occupied, and with the additional land across 34th Street we began the design of more doctors' offices at what is now Bailey Square.

Another new concept that doctors were talking about at the time was the outpatient surgical center. Half of the surgeries being done in hospitals at that time could have been done safely on an outpatient basis at one-third the cost, so we decided to make the top floor of the Bailey Square office building an outpatient surgical center. This new center had five operating rooms and eighteen pre-op rooms. It was the first of its kind in Texas, and it received national attention as an example of the best way to build such a facility.

We had plans for a nursing home adjacent to Bailey Square—actually a place somewhat like the early Westminster Manor—but the group couldn't come to a consensus on this idea.

The facilities we built in central Austin—Medical Park Tower, Shoal Creek Hospital, and Bailey Square—have now all been sold to other companies, and the area has attracted many other medical buildings. An initiative that originated as an idea by a small group for a new medical office building expanded dramatically into a major regional medical center.

"Mighty oaks from little acorns grow."

I NEVER LEARNED MUCH FROM MY SUCCESSES, ONLY FROM MY FAILURES:
WATCH OUT WHAT YOU ASK FOR—YOU MAY GET IT!

Theodore Reutz

I never learned much from my successes. I learned more from my mistakes. Some learning, like humility and handling my false pride, required multiple lessons.

As a result of my studies and experience at the Universidad Central de Venezuela (UCV) in Caracas, I suspected that problems of developing countries might have more to do with how they were governed than with economics. So I decided to change my focus from my undergraduate major in finance and economics to government studies and political economy. Therefore, after I received my MA from Stanford, I applied to the PhD program in the Department of Political Science.

Perhaps my newly assigned graduate advisor and I both showed excessive hubris. The advisor had me review some of my coursework, including the PhD sequence in economic development that I had just taken. Part I was taught by Professor Emile Despres, who had only an undergraduate degree and relied on Adam Smith and demand-and-supply curves. Part II was taught by Nobel Prize laureate and mathematical economist Kenneth J. Arrow. At the end of the year, we students voted on which professor had taught us the most. Depres, the professor *without* an advanced economics degree, was the overwhelming winner among these economics grad students whether they were math wizards or not. Since this advisor had asked, I shared the results of the student vote with him. He was not amused.

On the contrary, he said he doubted that I "was committed to the science of government and public policy, but rather wanted to become a US senator from Arkansas." I countered, "Even if I wanted to be a senator—which I do not—wouldn't study of public policy be a wonderful background?" Moreover, I continued, "I thought governing was an art" (as did Aristotle), not a science. He simply repeated his mantra that he wanted graduate students to be committed to developing "the science," as in "political science," and then he blocked my admission to Stanford. Fortunately, I had already applied and received a grant to attend graduate school at UCLA.

At UCLA I earned mostly straight As in the government department. I took a course from former governor Jerry Brown on how to run campaigns and put it to use doing paid political consulting. I did free consulting for the first Black candidate to run for Congress in eastern Arkansas and developed a complete campaign with ads, speeches, and billboards ("Hardy Croxton Will Fix This Pothole") for a congressional candidate in western Arkansas. My finest hour was probably when I urged him not to take out a second mortgage on his home. My research showed he could not win. I suggested that he withdraw. He took out the loan anyway and lost.

At UCLA I continued to exhibit false pride. First, on the written exam needed to advance to the PhD program, I felt that none of my answers represented my true brilliance, so I choked and was unable to complete the exam. Then, when key faculty members decided that because I had such high grades they would substitute an oral exam for the written exam I had freaked out on, what did I do? Rather than act appropriately thankful and modest, I was vain and overbearing. I could not continue in the PhD program.

Then, I believe what happened was this: My failure of choking on the MA exam at UCLA probably was not disclosed to other schools, since I already had a master's degree from Stanford, but that my almost-straight-A record did get reported. I received a tuition grant and a minor stipend to the University of Chicago, a university ranked above UCLA and Stanford in terms of its economics faculty (Nobel laureates), political philosophy (especially the study of Plato and Aristotle dealing with fundamental ideas of humanity like happiness, virtue, and justice), and public policy (Frederick Hayck and Milton Friedman, for example). I felt that I had failed upward.

At the University of Chicago, I was able to cover my living expenses while attending graduate school by substitute teaching in South Side ghetto housing projects. This proved more like a Hobbesian state of nature than anything I had experienced elsewhere. It was quite eventful. I had a second grader come after me with a knife, yelling, "I'll get you, you mother—er," and a third grader shouted similar obscenities as he brandished a two-by-four at me.

Because of social promotion policies, some of the seventh graders were fifteen or sixteen years old, quite large, and very frustrated in the ghetto schools. One day I walked into one such class just as a student threw an eraser at me. I lost it. I grabbed him and marched him down to the principal's office. The students themselves were impressed that I had removed the troublemaker. Guess what the principal told me? Not that it was good that I had removed the troublemaker, but that I should try to get along better with the students. As a substitute, the only way I could maintain any order at all was by playing *James Brown—Godfather of Soul* on the radio or record player and shutting it off in the event of serious disturbances.

From my experience in multiple ghetto schools, I concluded that teachers unions were focused on pay and were content to let young people graduate with no qualifications and no prospects of obtaining jobs. It is not surprising that much of today's gang violence comes from the South Side. My own apartment on South Fifty-seventh was robbed more than ten times in two years. One afternoon when I came home, an Indian gentleman was leaning out of a third-floor window, yelling in a high-pitched British accent, "Help! Help! These robbers mean to do me harm!" Another time, an ex-roommate of mine who drove up was accosted by two men who put a gun to his head and demanded, "Your billfold or your life!" It made you appreciate the Chicago police.

Despite the dangers, I loved the intellectual environment at the University of Chicago, where I studied political economy and public policy. My PhD committee was made up of professors from Economics, Government, and Philosophy. After my failed attempts to be brilliant on exams, I decided that this time I would focus on writing something that was "not stupid." I passed.

While I was still in graduate school I should have learned more about things like humility and virtue, but for the most part I did not. One lesson did begin to take root after the summer of 1968 when a friend of mine, Bill Coe, and I were sitting around a swimming pool in Little Rock drinking beer and attempting to figure out what we could do to earn money for the rest of the summer, since both of our political candidates had lost.

We came up with an idea of how to dampen votes for George Wallace by looking at specific counties in the South where other segregationist candidates had done well. (This was before widespread computer research.) We presented our idea to the president of Arkansas Louisiana Gas, who sent us to Dave Parr, the head of milk producers in more than eight states stretching from Minnesota and Wisconsin down to Arkansas and Louisiana. Parr thought he had found his own private brain trust, so he flew us down to HemisFair '68, the official 1968 World's Fair International Exposition in San Antonio, along with three thousand milk producers so we could have our picture made with the vice presidential candidate, Ed Muskie, and make our proposal to Muskie's staff. They signed on. Then Parr wanted to fly us to Washington, DC, to make our presentation. Our only question was who was paying for food and lodging. We were put up at the Mayflower Hotel with all bills paid. We were in.

There we met with senators, congressmen, and other officials, outlining for them what volunteers we would need: attorneys to study election codes, staff to research "stand-in-segregationist candidates" to substitute for George Wallace, clerical staff to research primary and general vote totals, staff to color in the county maps. We were given offices in the Watergate Building and were paid in excess of $10,000 each in today's dollars. Two days later, we had more than twenty-five volunteers working for us—attorneys, statisticians, and clerical staff.

If that wasn't enough to get the attention of a previously unemployed graduate student, there was more to heat up my hubris. I will always remember the result of my call to Mrs. J. Smith, head of volunteers on Connecticut Avenue. I thanked her for sending us all the great volunteers. Then I told her that what we really needed was one blonde and one brunette, five-five to five-seven, "who like to drink." After assuring her that I meant just "companionship," I expected that when the next blonde and the next brunette walked in, she would not be able to resist telling them to take five dollars and hail a cab to the Watergate Building so they could join Mr. Reutz and the volunteers.

When I returned to Little Rock, Dave Parr (aka Mr. Big) picked me up in his limo, debriefed me, and then threw me out on the sidewalk, stating (rightly) that I was one of the most arrogant, overbearing people he had ever had the displeasure to meet.

In what turned out to be an extreme case of watch-out-what-you-ask-for, I married the brunette. She definitely liked to drink. When we lived for three years in Buenos Aires, I would find empty vodka and gin bottles in our laundry hamper. When I naively asked where they came from and she answered, "I don't know." I must have been imbibing sufficient quantities of my own drug of choice (beer), since I simply let it go. We divorced, and she ultimately died of alcoholism.

After the divorce, an attorney friend of mine told me he thought it was a good time to challenge myself by taking EST training, as he had done. This was a two-weekend, fifty-hour course based on the human potential movement, Zen philosophy, transcendental meditation, and confrontation by workshop leaders. In one long meditation, we were asked to place ourselves back in high school and remember a time when we felt especially vulnerable. My guided meditation took me back to a test in third-year Latin. I was perspiring profusely and thinking that if I did well, I would likely get into Harvard (and show my father up, since he had had only one year of college). But if I did poorly, my mother would not love me. Then, still in the meditation, we were instructed to go back to middle school. I remembered being at summer camp. My parents were driving out to visit me, and I was in a cross-country race, telling myself that I was going to win it so my parents would love me.

Then we were asked to carry the same sense of vulnerability back to when we were four or five years old. This time I remembered that my father had come home drunk after a contractors' meeting, and my mother and father woke me up with their yelling. I ran into the kitchen and saw my father choking my mother and her picking up a butcher knife. The two most important people in my world were going to wipe each other out! I got between them and pushed them apart. Apparently, I decided that through my efforts, I could solve their relationship and find love for myself. Heavy delusions for a child.

In another exercise, we were led through a three-hour meditation and then asked to focus on "an item" that we wanted to work on. Many people said they wanted to overcome "fear of failure." At the next break I shared with a female participant that an effort to overcome fear of failure did not seem crucial to me, since in my life failure had generally been a good thing. I had failed upward from working as a volunteer for defeated candidates to a lucrative post at the national level, and I had failed upward to the University of Chicago. This lady immediately said, "What about fear of success, gaining everything you want—love, money, whatever?" Fear of success seemed dumb but felt right, so I entered the next guided meditation with that as "my item."

The meditation that followed was transformational. I remembered a cartoon I had read showing a man and his young son in a small rowboat next to a big yacht that towered over them. The man was saying, "Look, that yacht owner has probably used up all his potential (working to get that yacht) while I am still saving my potential." I also remembered a scene from an Argentinian movie in which José San Martín, one of the liberators of South America, appeared in a vision to a group of exiles and said, "Decide. Decide. Decision Is Already Success." I decided that if the universe wanted to bestow half a million dollars in earnings per year on me and provide love and affection, I would be open to it. It did not happen overnight, but my transformation began.

My next step was even more transformational. It was a Christian-based spiritual retreat more than sixty miles north of Montreal. In order to attend, I had to fill out a questionnaire about my character defects and life concerns. Dave Parr, who had kicked me out of his limo, had been correct. Now I self-identified that I was an overbearing alcoholic with inflated self-importance. In the role-playing exercises at the retreat, I was selected by sixteen of twenty participants to portray their overbearing father cursing them. Subsequently, I was sent out "to talk to a tree" for two hours and come back not with what I believed in—people believe in lots of things, like money, power, sex, drugs— but a definition of what I had faith in. What kind of a tree would you choose to talk to? I chose a white poplar tree and brought back this definition from my encounter with it: "I have faith in that which is highest in my fellow man and in myself, linked to the natural order of things under God." I still feel centered as I type this.

We were also encouraged to come up with personal prayers or affirmations to counteract our character defects. My affirmations included:

> I stop false pride, I start humility.
> I stop grandiose illusions, I accept reality.
> I stop drinking, I start exercising.
> I forgive myself, I forgive myself ——— (fill in for what).
> I stop self-pity, I start self-actualization.

The good news is that I have not drugged or drunk alcohol in the more than thirty years since. During the monthlong retreat, I went swimming every day in the cold Canadian water and repeated my affirmations. To this day, when I want to discharge negative self-talk and negative feelings, I go swimming and repeat selected prayers and affirmations.

Even my modified grandiose illusions have been useful in certain circumstances. First, when I formed an employee-benefits business, I flew over to Lloyd's of London on my own dime to investigate how a Fortune 500 company might obtain medical coverage for US civilians working in a war zone. Not something that someone focused on humility would have done, given that the national insurance advisors to the 40,000-employee company had been unsuccessful in gaining coverage during the war in Bosnia. But I was able to create a type of pour-over contract stating that losses in one area could be made up in another. I also developed competitive bids to secure medical and life insurance coverage for more than 20,000 employees who were working abroad.

Second, although my grand illusions led me to make some bad investments in real estate, they may have been partly responsible for my digging out. Four of the six men with whom I was jointly and severally liable for a shopping center declared bankruptcy, leaving just two of us holding the bag. This was 1986 and banks were failing left and right, so even the bank in question did not press us into bankruptcy, instead settling for two cents on the dollar, deferred and paid over time. Moreover, the agreement stipulated that I could not settle with any other financial institution for more than two cents. If I did, I would have to declare bankruptcy. That bank transferred its losses to the FDIC. You can settle a lot of debt at two cents paid over time.

However, I also owned numerous rental houses that had been foreclosed on. I was able to save this bank more than the $300,000 I owed on the foreclosures by restructuring its employee benefits with greater employee choice. The bank president wrote off my $300,000 debt, and I felt like I had turned lemons into lemonade.

Pretty neat. I did not have to declare bankruptcy.

As I learned to control my false pride, I was able to build a wonderful relationship with Jackie Balven, the woman I married and have loved deeply for more than twenty-five years. I found out there is a thin line between success and failure. I was also able to develop a successful business and lecture on public policy and health care reform at the University of Texas at Austin.

All in all, I can definitely say that throughout my life I have learned more from my failures than from my successes.

BLAME IT ON THE HARDY BOYS

Mike Roche

Doors and passages hidden behind grandfather clocks and bookcases excited my ten-year-old mind when I first encountered brothers Frank and Joe Hardy and their chum, Chet. In fact—and my friends will attest to this—I still have an affinity for things secret: velvet-lined jewelry compartments in vanities and shallow drawers in desks that might hold gold coins, silver storage behind pressure-sensitive wall panels in grand dining rooms, and doors that aren't doors.

My godmother, whom we all called "Aunt Jessie," was my grandmother's best friend, and my mother was very fond of her. So, when I was born, my mom asked Aunt Jessie to be my godmother.

Aunt Jessie was a dear. She was an avid reader, and about the time I turned ten, books replaced toys as her favorite gifts to me. Early on, Aunt Jessie introduced me to author Franklin W. Dixon and the Hardy Boys series. I was proud to have my very own copy of *The Disappearing Floor*—or was it *The Secret Panel*?

The stories were action-packed, nonstop adventures. Frank and Joe were amateur detectives, eager to assist their attorney father in solving crimes. The stories often started with "a speeding car" and quickly involved long-abandoned mansions with hidden rooms or storied treasures lost in tunnels beneath piles of crumbling walls, but they always ended with good outdoing evil.

(Much to my surprise, I found out in later years that "Franklin W. Dixon" was not the author's real name, nor was the series written by a single author. The Hardy Boys series was produced by numerous ghostwriters but always followed a storyline created by Edward Stratemeyer, owner of the Stratemeyer Syndicate, which also published the Nancy Drew series and others.)

This fascination with concealed doors, secret drawers, and hidden panels has stayed with me for all these years, and it has been an enjoyable pastime when visiting antique stores or touring American mansions or European castles.

A visit to Ireland's Birr Castle is still my best experience of exploring for secret rooms and secret passages.

Gayle and I, with our good friends Roy and Erin, were on a National Trust tour of Western Ireland. We overnighted at various manor houses and grand estates, but I found my secrets in a castle that was hundreds of years old and still occupied by descendants of the founder.

Birr Castle became famous mostly because of a very large astronomical telescope that was completed in 1845. Scientists from around the globe came to study far distances and to create their own scientific works.

The observatory, gardens and chapel were included in our castle tour, as was a luncheon with an heir. Our group was in the main dining room, and while being served, I rather flippantly asked the waiter about "the secret panels."

"Oh, they're all in the library," he replied.

I could feel the thrill. I couldn't finish lunch quickly enough. I had to get to the library before our tour continued. I had to look for telltale signs of concealed secrets. A clue might come from a tiny gap in the wood molding around the bookcases or the wainscoting, possibly revealing an entry point. Push, pull, or slide? My first two tries were disappointments and simply opened into hallways. But the third try was the charm!

The door was in the bookcase, to the right of the marble fireplace. My heart rate increased by several beats as I gently pulled on a section of the book filled wall and it moved. Inside was a tiny room, lighted and with walls upholstered in light green fabric. Opposite my entry point was another door, providing an exit. I stepped through the small space and exited into a beautifully appointed large drawing room, not realizing that the exit door had quietly closed behind me. At that same moment, I could hear our tour guide explaining our host's family history while he led our group through the public rooms, headed my way. If I were found in the drawing room ahead of the tour, I would be embarrassed. I'd be exposed as a snoop.

When I turned to leave, there was no door! The group was about to enter the drawing room, and I was about to be humiliated.

Where the door should have been stood a breakfront, formidable in size and filled with fragile and highly prized contents. Displayed through glass doors were arrays of ornamental plates, saucers, and dainty cups, all collected by our host's ancestors over the centuries. The center console was topped by a broken pediment, and each flanking cabinet was crowned with a large decorative pottery urn.

Cleverly, the door I needed turned out to be the cabinet section nearest to me and fortunately this side of the breakfront swung open easily. I retraced my steps and caught up with our group just as they entered the drawing room. Our tour ended with a walk through the observatory and the gardens with a glimpse of the chapel.

I've heard that the intriguing part of the castle is the passage leading out to the chapel. Oh, how I wish . . .

But I know those Hardy Boys could have had plenty of fun exploring all the nooks and crannies at Birr Castle.

A YEAR AT CALTECH

Sam Sampson

In 1957 I began the fall semester of my second year at McCormick Theological Seminary in Chicago with two major expectations: (1) I had married Lois, and I expected a lasting marriage, and (2) I would graduate in May of 1959. The marriage did not last, and I did not graduate until 1960. What follows is the account of how my senior year was delayed by an internship at Caltech, officially the California Institute of Technology.

I learned that the Danforth Foundation was accepting applications for second-year seminarians to spend a year in an internship program at a college or university under the supervision of a college chaplain. I applied, which led to an interview with a Danforth official. In December I received a letter saying I had been accepted and assigned to Caltech. I assumed that my major in mathematics at Iowa State University may have influenced my placement.

During the Christmas break I shared my news with Bill Anderson, my college roommate, and learned that he had been accepted at Caltech in the Aeronautical Engineering PhD program. It was good to know that Bill and his wife, Betty, would be there with Lois and me.

In mid-August there was an orientation in Michigan. There were eleven interns, with a supervisor from each participating university and a faculty member from each intern's seminary. Robert Rankin, the Danforth Foundation coordinator, was accompanied by a senior member of the foundation. Several of us were married, and our wives were also included in the orientation.

For me the most important part was meeting my supervisor, Wes Hershey, the general secretary of the Caltech YMCA and the only supervisor who was not a chaplain. He put me at ease immediately. The senior Danforth official arrived with a wood carving of two figures. The top part was the head of a father with a benign expression, one hand resting lovingly on the head of a son in front of him. The son had an anguished expression on his face, for the father's other hand was around the son's neck. It was titled *Paternalism*, and each intern was given an 8" x 10" photo of it.

In a private moment with me, Wes commented on the irony—he thought the Danforth Foundation was not exempt from paternalism. The interns had met with this official, urging that future orientations be held at the end of August so that summer jobs would not be interrupted. I told Wes that the official was glad to hear what we had said and would certainly take it into consideration. However, the reservations for the next year had already been made. Wes laughed and said, "Every year interns make the same request, and get the same answer." While the Danforth Foundation was generous, it did prefer to follow the pattern that it had established.

Our main obligation to Danforth was to write a letter each month discussing whatever we chose. We also received $25 the first month to spend for our ministry with students. In order to get $25 for .the next month and subsequent months, we had to report how we had used the current month's money.

By the time Lois and I left for California, we had learned that she was pregnant. Thus our year quickly gained additional challenges and anticipations. We drove cross-country to Pasadena. Wes had arranged a rental apartment for us, since housing became scarcer as the beginning of the academic year approached. I had contacted the Andersons and asked if they would like us to find a place for them as well, since we would be arriving two weeks before they did. They agreed, and we soon appreciated even more what Wes had done for us. We eventually located the home of a retired couple who were traveling for a year, and they consented to rent it to Bill and Betty.

Caltech has always been very selective, and it remains so; currently, it accepts less than 4 percent of applicants. In 1958–59, there were 700 undergraduates, 550 graduate students, and 400 faculty. I attended the orientation retreat for freshmen. On the first night students shared high school accomplishments. By the next day no one was talking about high school. Everyone was already caught up in what lay ahead. They were expected to follow the honor code and to strive for excellence. All of these students had been at or near the top of their high school classes. Now half of them would be in the bottom half of the class. If their self-esteem had centered on doing well academically, this change in class ranking could be stressful.

A major emphasis for Wes was making sure that the Caltech Y was welcoming to students and supportive of them. The fact that all of the students were academically gifted didn't mean that they were immune to the challenges of Caltech or those of their ongoing progress toward independence. Conflict with parents was an issue for many of them; interpersonal communication was another. Some had concentrated so much on science that they had neglected to develop many social skills.

There were four people at Caltech who still have significant places in my memory. Wes Hershey, my supervisor, was the most influential. In 1946 he had begun what would be a thirty-year tenure at the Caltech Y. He had established a good relationship with the founding president of Caltech, Robert Millikan, who left a bequest to help fund programs at the Y. Wes, a gentle Quaker, saw the best in everyone. There were no religious services. Wes acknowledged that some programs might deal with religion, but he did so reluctantly. He believed that religion was not really a separate discipline, but a part of everything that happens. Programs that he had developed increased awareness of ethical issues and concerns in a variety of ways.

Wes frequently sat down with me to reflect on meetings, especially those that involved controversy or conflict. Why had the group so strongly resisted ideas presented by a particular student? What had we learned about the members of the group? Most important, he sought my input to evaluate our own leadership. What did we do that helped the group move ahead? What had we learned about ourselves? In his gentle manner, he helped me seek improvement. This has been a lasting gift, as I reflect on what I learn about and from others, and what I continue to learn about myself.

Sylvia, an immigrant from Switzerland, was the secretary at the Y. She was one of the few women with whom students had regular contact. Working in an all-male environment, Sylvia exhibited a wonderfully direct style. She did not put up with any nonsense. She was respectful but not overawed by men, even those who had won a Nobel Prize.

Wes often asked Sylvia to compose his letters. The Y had a small loan program, and some students had to be reminded to make their payments. Wes sometimes had Sylvia redo a letter to soften the language. One day when she brought a letter for his signature, she commented, "I was really nice this time." Wes read the letter, laughed, and wrote, "Sylvia composed this letter. I would have used more gentle language, but I concur with what she says." Then he signed it.

Students viewed the theoretical physicist Richard Feynman as a hero, and they persuaded me to attend one of his lectures. When I did so, it was easy to see why he was so well regarded. In the classroom he was part lecturer and part stand-up comedian. There was more levity in that one lecture than in all the Iowa State physics classes I had taken—all to help students gain understanding and appreciate the mystery of quantum mechanics. One of Feynman's famous quotes is "If you think you understand quantum mechanics, you don't understand quantum mechanics." This sounds like a parallel to theologians who say, "If you think you understand God, you don't understand God." Caltech students not only found Feynman a wonderful teacher but loved his capricious nature. He wrote of the night in 1965 when his phone rang at 3:00 a.m. When he returned to the bedroom his wife asked, "What was that all about?" He replied that he had won the Nobel Prize in Physics. Thoroughly inured to his off-the-wall comments, she responded, "Yeah . . . right," turned over, and went back to sleep.

Of all the students, the most memorable was Tom—a math major who ranked second academically in the senior class. Tom organized a T. S. Eliot weekend retreat and enlisted an English professor to provide leadership. About twenty people participated, including several young women invited by Caltech students, and a YMCA trustee made available a large home in Laguna Beach. It was a stimulating and fun weekend, discussing T. S. Eliot and taking breaks on the beach.

Campus culture at Caltech was both typical and unique. Many students headed to the athletic fields late in the afternoon to play intramural or varsity sports. About 80 percent of the football players had not lettered in high school. Caltech students had pilfered a stone marker from Occidental College and set it up like a grave marker on the Caltech campus. Later, three Caltech students were caught on the Occidental campus and given free haircuts—all the hair on their heads was removed except for one letter on each head: an O, an X, and a Y. In another prank, some students made sure no one slept through a final exam by setting speakers in the window and playing Wagner's "Ride of the Valkyries" at high volume at 6:00 a.m. on exam days.

Because there were no women students on campus at that time, dating was a challenge. One student concluded that "maybe explaining the Heisenberg uncertainty principle isn't the best way to impress a date." The campaign for student elections included short speeches, but the main attraction was two striptease dancers hired for the occasion.

Campus culture has changed since then. In 1970 Caltech began admitting women, who now make up 45 percent of the student body. While many referred to the "Y" when I was there, that abbreviated designation is now official. The Caltech YMCA has dropped the "MCA," and its executive director is a woman.

Over the years Wes created several important programs, one of which was Leaders of America. A leader in some field was brought to the campus to engage directly with students. Abraham Maslow, a psychologist who developed a theory that humans develop through a hierarchy of needs, was greeted enthusiastically and responded by generously extending his time with the students. I recall one night when after an evening gathering, he went out with students for a late meal, then found another group waiting when he returned.

Another of Wes's programs was Visiting Seminarians. He invited seminaries to send a top senior student for a week of engagement with Caltech students. The one rabbinical student who participated had especially vigorous conversations— Jewish students who were raised without religious practices, as well as those who rebelled against such practices, wanted to talk.

The Jewish theologian Will Herberg was another of the guests. I remember him sitting on the edge of his chair in our living room like an intellectual pugilist, ready to take on any argument. Students seemed to respond well to his aggressive style.

One recurring issue was how scientists should be involved in public policy. Some argued that scientists should stick to discovering, and leave how discoveries were used to the public and the politicians. Others believed scientists were in the best position to educate people. Faculty members were active in opposing atomic testing and were writing about the dangers of population explosion, a major factor in climate change.

We once held a joint faculty and student retreat with Scripps College for Women. It was modestly titled "The Intellectual's Responsibility to Society." One speaker identified three stages that can describe many issues. The first involves a discovery that does good; the second arises when money can be made producing or using the discovery; the third when there may be bad consequences. He used DDT as an example. We could use the internet, social media, capitalism, or petroleum as well. Almost any creative human endeavor can have good or bad effects. The challenge is to learn and correct for negative consequences, complicated by the fact that those who are making money or who are otherwise privileged tend to resist change.

The retreat was lively, and conversations spun off in many directions. I heard one animated exchange in which Caltech students were trying to convince women that expressing an atomic relationship in a formula was an aesthetic experience just as much as music or art. On the way back from the retreat, a Caltech student said he had dated two of the women, but got to know them better at the retreat than he ever had on dates.

These and other Y programs offered ample opportunity for me to interact with students. I also provided study materials for those who wanted to discuss topics such as current plays or existentialism.

Lois and I were asked to host three students from Hawaii who were arriving early for a Y conference between Christmas and New Year's. They were delightful young men, and we enjoyed showing them around the Los Angeles area. At the close of our time with them, the uncle and aunt they were staying with invited us to be their guests for a Christmas Eve dinner at a restaurant. On the way, the uncle asked if we had been told that the students were Japanese. We said no. He expressed surprise. We learned that the uncle had been confined in an internment camp in the US during World War II and expected that many white people would be reluctant to host Japanese students.

During that end-of-year break all the interns, supervisors, and seminary faculty gathered in St. Louis. Each intern reported on his experience, and his remarks were followed by his supervisor's comments. It was interesting to hear these summaries, but it took up nearly all the meeting time and got a bit tedious. More importantly, there were some concerns that could not be dealt with by forty people. A few interns had had conflicts with their supervisors—in one case, a very serious conflict.

The final event on the agenda was reminiscing about the orientation in August, but in a minor rebellion, the interns announced that they needed to meet separately during that last time slot. It seemed important for us to hear from those who were having a difficult time

At Caltech I was challenged to deal with both informed and naive religious skepticism. I found people who admired Reinhold Niebuhr's political thinking, but not his theological foundation. I became more aware of international issues and environmental concerns, and was influenced to move politically toward Democrats. After hearing people talk about Richard Nixon's early career, I knew I could not vote for him. I expect that those same people were not surprised by Watergate.

I was so impressed with the preaching of Ganse Little at the Pasadena Presbyterian Church that Lois and I attended services there almost every Sunday. I remember only one sermon, however. Ganse Little was preaching on the theological significance of names and identity, and made the assertion that men should be aware that women were giving up a lot when they agreed to take a man's name in marriage. That idea stuck with me over the years. The traditional pattern seemed to suggest that a woman's identity changes with marriage, while the man's does not. Years later, when Ellen Babinsky and I were in an earnest discussion of whether we would marry, Ellen said, "I won't be taking your name." My response was immediate: "Is that a yes?" It was.

At a program for college students at Pasadena Presbyterian, we were surprised to hear that the speaker was a Beatnik. Only at the end of the session did we learn that he was actually a campus minister from San Francisco who was taking on the persona of a Beatnik. One result was that I acquired books by Allen Ginsberg and Lawrence Ferlinghetti.

In March our daughter, Roberta, was born. A surprise baby shower for Lois at Wes Hershey's home provided many of the necessities for taking care of a newborn. I had to learn the art of diapering and a lot more.

Our last gathering with students was at Bill and Betty's home. It was our last time with Tom. Some six months later I learned that he was in a mathematics PhD program at the University of Chicago. He was still dealing with conflict with his parents and was trying to take some English courses. At the end of the meeting Tom took Robbie while Lois and I said good-bye to folks. When we were ready to leave, we found a very contented baby in Tom's arms listening to his version of a lullaby. He was singing "One for the baby, and one more for the road."

Very soon we were on the road, driving from Pasadena to Westhope, North Dakota, where I served the Presbyterian church there for the summer—a bit of a culture shock after Caltech—and then returned to McCormick for my senior year.

After my intern experience I brought a more critical evaluation of ideas to my classes. I would sometimes write "Caltech?" as I took notes. That made some ideas more relevant, and some not so much. Being in an all-male environment at Caltech had made me more open to feminist concerns for women's equality. I came back with a larger worldview, aware of many more challenges. The year at Caltech was a vital part of my education and life.

THE DAY WE BURIED MOTHER

Phyllis Schenkkan

Yes, she was a difficult woman—conTRARy, her surviving sister and brothers and her husband would have said. In life, she taught English, French, and Latin, and spoke, read, and wrote Finnish fluently, but taught no foreign languages to her children. She was a good cook and a brilliant baker. She sewed beautifully, but never finished a garment. (I learned to sew because I was tired of being pinned into my dresses!) And in my memory, Mother rarely spent a day without a temper tantrum. That has to be an inflated memory; I loathed quarreling. Mother's favorite activity to cool down from her anger was to rake the barnyard until it looked beautiful, the lines in the dirt and gravel symmetrical and clear. She was a smart, capable, and difficult woman, a problematic role model with a wicked sense of humor. She was funny! But even Mother, contrary as she was, couldn't have predicted this day.

Winter in northern Ohio is cold and often slushy. After being excused from jury duty in February 2001, I flew to Cleveland and drove to Barberton so I could take Aunt Alma, whom the fifteen cousins called "Everybody's Favorite Aunt," to the funeral. On Sunday, February 25, 2001, we made our way to the old Route 5 and Ravenna, Ohio, where Mother had lived for a number of years—the town where she was born, the town we went through every two weeks when we were young to visit our Finnish grandparents and our cousins. Most of the relatives lived on the west side of this small but prosperous community.

On this day I started to go to the stately Wood Funeral Home on Main Street, where all the other family funerals had been held, but Alma stopped me—Mother was being interred from the new funeral home. She had made the order. That begins to tell you a little bit more about Mother. Contrary?

Oh, yes, the orders: No funeral service at Wood Funeral Home ("I don't like that place") and especially no church-oriented service ("I'm an atheist—no Bible reading"); no viewing (a custom from the Lutheran Church, which Mother, along with the other Finns on Red Brush Road, was raised in). Perhaps a dozen of us gathered: only Mother's half-sister, Aunt Alma, and her sister-in-law, Gertie Kaupinen, from her generation; my sister, Jean; my brother, Tom; and a few cousins. It was a treat to see the cousins, and there was always a lot of time spent reminiscing about the fun we had at Mumma's—our grandmother's—farm.

And there was the open casket: Mother's hair was curled, heavy makeup had been applied, and she wore her best dress. Tom, an evangelical church pastor, and his fellow minister presided over the service. Uh-oh! Here was the last of Mother's claims to have control over what was to ensue. The service for the handful of us was filled with biblical readings, prayers, and guarantees of a place in heaven for her. I could feel Mother's ire from afar. My sister, too, was aghast: "What is Tom doing?"

Then off we went to the beautiful old Maple Grove Cemetery, where family members had been buried since 1906. Mother's father died of pneumonia when she was two years old. Later, her half-brother, Allan Wakkila, and sister Lily Kaupinen died in the 1920s tuberculosis epidemic, and they were buried there, as were other family members. We had driven every Memorial Day from our farm in Newton Falls, twenty-five miles away, to place flowers on the graves. But memory intervenes; that's what homecoming does. Back to the story—we have turned into the cemetery.

"Wait!" Alma exclaimed. "You're going right past the family plot."

"I know, but I'm following Tom and the funeral car."

"But our plot is right there at the front of the cemetery!" On we went, following Tom and the casket.

We stopped at the very back of the cemetery. Tom and the funeral director got out of their cars, walked over to a prepared gravesite (the hole in the ground), and talked and talked, very seriously. I waited and waited. Alma became more and more upset, so I finally went over to join them.

Oops! There seemed to be some confusion. The space for the coffin that was to be buried at this site had a headstone with a name that began with "S," a Middle European name. No Kaupinen or Wakkila here! More discussion. Finally, the funeral director decided there was nothing to be done but to look at our family plot. Back to the front of the cemetery we went, only to see that there was a freshly filled-in gravesite. No empty hole. No space to bury Mother. Someone else had mistakenly been buried in our plot! More discussion. Phone calls.

An additional complication. Somehow, the "S" family had not noticed they were in the wrong place or that the names on the headstones were not their family names; however, they were Roman Catholic, and the funeral home could not move the body without permission from the priest at the local church. More delay. What to do?

Oddly, Tom had not arranged a reception of any kind. So here he was, on Sunday afternoon, looking around for a place where we could wait out the exhumation of one body so we could inter another. The only place open was East Park Restaurant, a truck stop that had been there forever, famous for its hamburgers and liver and onions. Family had grabbed a bite there for years. It was now about two in the afternoon, and no one had had lunch, so away we went to East Park Restaurant. We had lunch, told family stories, and waited. And waited. And waited. Now there were only half a dozen of us. Most of the cousins had had to go home.

The phone call came. The priest had done whatever needed to be done, and the "S" body had been disinterred and moved. And now the coffin bearing Edna Kaupinen Thomas could be properly buried at the family site. Even on the day we buried her, Mother had managed to make her personality felt—conTRARy to the end!

THE GRAVEYARD EASTER

Judy Skaggs

When my friend Kathy told our small group that she had been diagnosed with a lung disease that would end her life in just a few years, we were shocked and tremendously saddened. But the way Kathy faced her illness and ultimate death taught those of us who were privileged to be with her a great deal about both living and dying.

At one point she brought us a song, "Dance in the Graveyards." It spoke to the way she felt about dying. The chorus goes like this:

When I die
I don't want to rest in peace
I want to dance in joy
I want to dance in the graveyards, the graveyards
And while I'm alive
I don't want to be alone
Mourning the ones who came before
I want to dance with them some more
Let's dance in the graveyards

The song was such a gift to us, just as Kathy had so often gifted us in the past. Kathy's way of dealing with living and dying reminded me of another time I had learned about life and death, but in a most unusual way. Thinking about these lessons brought back memories of something that happened in my childhood.

I grew up in the small West Texas town of Eldorado. By "small," I mean population 2,400 on a good day. A small town is a great place to grow up. Everyone knows everyone, which, of course, can be both good and bad. There were only twenty-eight kids in my graduating class, so we knew one another very well.

Small towns are sometimes known for their "characters," and almost everyone had a nickname. For instance, there was Bob "Pitcher" Page. When the kids would gather on the vacant lot in our neighborhood to play baseball, Pitcher would be the only one who had a ball, and he wouldn't play unless he got to be the pitcher.

Mr. and Mrs. Carson West could also be described as small-town characters. They had no children of their own, so they sort of adopted a lot of us kids. Their big old farmhouse on the edge of town was a magical place for children. They had guinea pigs and rabbits, goats and bantam hens and roosters, and a huge parrot that lived in the big tree out in front. Whenever someone drove up, that parrot would start squawking: "Carson! Carson! Someone's here!!!"

Around Christmastime, the Wests would cut one of the big cedar trees in the pasture, bring it up to the house, and invite several families to come over and help trim it with decorations that we made: paper chains, strings of popcorn and cranberries, and cut-out tinfoil stars.

But the most unusual thing Mrs. West did was to have an Easter egg hunt on the Saturday before Easter at the local cemetery. I grew up during the drought, so the cemetery was dry and dusty, and the grass was mostly brown. There were a few mesquite trees scattered around, but overall it was a pretty gray place.

When we arrived, we could see brightly colored eggs on some of the tombstones. Those eggs added life to the gray tombstones and the brown grass. We would gather around one of the graves and pick up the eggs. Then Mrs. West would tell us a story about the person buried there, about how the person lived and contributed to our little community. She would often tell us something a bit unexpected, like it was a secret. I remember that one time we stopped at Mrs. Royster's grave, and I was surprised to read on her marker that she and I had the same birthday. Mrs. West also told me that Mrs. Royster had been my daddy's second-grade teacher. I've never forgotten that. Then we would move on to the next grave for another story.

I'm not sure Mrs. West knew what she was teaching us, and I'm sure that as children, we did not understand it. But as I think back to that time, I realize she was teaching us not to be afraid of the graveyard. There were no ghosts or goblins there—instead it was a place of memories, of stories, of love. She wanted us to know that the people buried there would never be forgotten. Their stories would live on in our memories. She taught us that life and death are very connected, and that death is not to be feared. As we hunted Easter eggs in the cemetery, we were celebrating the mystery of Easter morning, when life overcomes death. I'm so grateful for her gift to us—something that we would remember all our lives.

LAW AND ORDER

Bill Strong

"Jerry! Haven't seen you for a while. Where have you been?" Jerry was a shipmate on the *USS Salem*. "I'm on permanent Shore Patrol. Just came aboard to get some clean skivvies. Two weeks done and two weeks to go. You should try it, Bill. It's a sweet deal. If you want it next, see Mr. Jenkins." Jerry said he was the rider on the Shore Patrol (SP) paddy wagon working from midnight to 8 a.m. When a ship enters port, petty officers are assigned rotations on Shore Patrol. Their job is to keep their shipmates out of trouble while ashore. I was on SP dozens of times in my thirty months of sea duty.

Jerry's suggestion was most interesting! Christmas was two weeks away. Since October the *Salem* had been in dry dock at the Navy Yard in Charlestown, Massachusetts. Exasperated by the dry dock turmoil, roaring blowers, and the incessant thrumming of twenty thousand tons of steel, I would leap at almost any opportunity for a bit of tranquility; so I volunteered. Late one afternoon in mid-December, I shouldered my seabag, walked down the gangway, along the dry dock, past "Old Ironsides," out the gate, and under the elevated tracks to the YMCA, where I got a room for a couple of bucks a night.

Shortly before midnight I entered the Permanent Shore Patrol office in the basement of the Joy Street police station. There I reported to the chief petty officer and met my new boss, Ernie, the paddy wagon driver. Chief was an elderly gentleman of forty or fifty years. Ernie, like me, was a 3rd class petty officer, but the two hash marks on his sleeve indicated over six years of service. The paddy wagon turned out to be a 1948 Dodge panel truck. Cyclone fencing demarcated the cargo area. Rear seating consisted of pine planks. Color scheme throughout was battleship gray. Under the dashboard a small heater provided air conditioning.

On our first mission, we brought back SPs finishing their downtown shifts. The office was quiet until Chief's phone rang. There was a ruckus at a social club near the Bunker Hill monument. This time it wasn't the Redcoats. It was the residue of a Christmas party for the crew of an LST (Landing Ship, Tank). A few revelers were celebrating in the street. Most conspicuously, one barefooted seaman was cursing and threatening all in sight. We got him into the van and were about to leave when a Lieutenant JG ordered us to release the sailor and vacate the truck so that the JG could entertain his new girlfriend in our cargo area. Ernie demurred. The guards at the Navy Yard gate were concerned about noises they said they had heard coming from the truck. Ernie managed to finesse us through, thus saving the unshod desperado to face his own skipper's justice. Once on the pier, our wheels crunched through thick snow for a quarter mile down to the LST's gangway. The Officer of the Deck sent two men out to collect the kid, last seen barefoot in snow up to his ankles, still hollering and challenging, oblivious to chill and common sense.

Each night ended with a tour of jails holding sailors arrested by the local police, almost always for drunken behavior. Inevitably, I found the miscreant sleeping in a cell. I awakened him with a gentle tap of the nightstick on the sole of the shoe, helped him up, and walked him to the truck for his ride back to his ship.

Not long after the LST party, on an even wintrier night, Chief dispatched us to an address on Essex Street which turned out to be a tall parking garage. Out in the street, the manager flagged us down and shouted "He's here. Just swing right in." Ernie backed the truck into the garage alongside the office entrance. I opened the cargo doors and stepped into the office to confront a very frightened, a very cold, and a very naked seventeen-year-old boy.

Fresh from boot camp and flush with eight weeks' pay, Jimmy had arrived that day for ship assignment at the Fargo Building—the US Naval Receiving Station. By evening he had made his way to the infamous "Combat Zone," a warren of dives that pandered to sailors. In one such establishment, he was charmed by two young ladies who offered to take him to a better place. Around four in the morning the manager found him sleeping in the back seat of a car parked on the fifth floor of the garage.

I got him up onto a plank bench in the back of the truck, slammed the doors, and headed to the Fargo Building—the shivering kid howling all the way. The entrance was right on the sidewalk, perhaps thirty feet from the curb. Unfortunately, a Checker Cab with a flat tire blocked our way. In the cab were several telephone operators coming off shift. In consideration of the tender sensibilities of the ladies, Ernie wouldn't let me take the kid across the sidewalk. It took me some time to locate a blanket for the boy, but we finally got him to his temporary home.

My month away from the *Salem* cured my dockyard blues, and we were soon on our way to "Gitmo"—Guantanamo Bay, the big fleet anchorage and training center at the eastern tip of Cuba. Routine maintenance and drills kept us busy. One evening I drew Beach Guard duty; that is, I ushered sailors on and off the launches that carried liberty parties to and from the shore. Around midnight at the fleet landing, I heard some all-too-familiar voices that heralded the arrival of two seventeen-year-olds from my division: Frenchy Guidry from Plaquemine Parish, Louisiana, and Jesse Van Dyke of Sand Hill, Virginia. What I liked most about them was that they didn't work for me. "Bill you gotta help us! You gotta arrest that guy! He beat Jesse up with his stick and knocked him down." A red knot decorated Jesse's forehead. Standing nearby was a fellow second class petty officer, an SP from another ship. Curiously, he seemed uninterested in the drama he had provoked. I loaded the boys into the *Salem*'s launch. Off duty and back aboard, I found a small audience watching the victim's poignant re-creation of the atrocity. It might have been more convincing had an eyewitness not whispered that Jesse had walked into a tree branch and had been helped to his feet by the petty officer.

After my third Mediterranean cruise, I transferred to the Fargo Building for an early discharge. This headquarters building had barracks for 8,000 sailors. It could accommodate whole crews of ships under construction or repair, sailors waiting for reassignment, or goodness knows what else. On October 31, with discharge papers in hand, I was the last man on a short line of soon-to-be-freed sailors. I felt a none-too-gentle tap on my shoulder and was led from the line to discover that I had been selected for a special, important national defense mission that would utilize my expertise in electronics and gunnery.

I was to spend one more month in the US Navy as a Master of Arms supervising the mess hall chow line—my final act as a dispenser of military justice.

MY AMERICAN ROOTS: CROSS-CULTURAL MARRIAGE

Mani Subramanian

My life in America moved fast, laying footprints and setting roots after I arrived from India in 1959 to pursue a graduate program at Purdue University in West Lafayette, Indiana. I progressed academically by earning a doctoral degree, adapted socially to the American lifestyle partly by being informally adopted by an American family through a Purdue program, and advanced professionally by holding summer research jobs. In the summer of 1961, I worked at Zenith Radio Corporation in Chicago, where a Purdue colleague introduced me to Ruth Pressler, who was his girlfriend and a secretary at Zenith. He asked her to help me since I was a foreign student from India. She did—and continues to do so to this day.

My relationship with Ruth began innocently enough: I started giving her rides to and from work every day. As the summer progressed, I mentioned that I missed playing tennis. She expressed interest in learning the game. So we started playing tennis some evenings. I did not know then that she had an interest in learning more than tennis. After that summer she never played again.

Ruth was born and grew up in Chicago, which is about 130 miles from West Lafayette. On the weekends, she took me to the city's popular tourist places, among them the Art Institute and the Museum of Science and Industry. We often walked on a Lake Michigan beach and had long talks about our families and our religious beliefs. Ruth was raised as a Baptist and was still a practicing Christian; her primary interest was singing in the church choir. I was raised as a Hindu Brahmin with a strong belief in Hindu philosophy, but not in the rituals—especially the caste system. Our curiosity took us to visit the Baha'i Temple to explore its teachings about the unity of God, the unity of religion, and the unity of humanity.

By the end of summer, we had become close friends, and I asked Ruth out on a formal date. I had never dated a girl in my two years in America, nor in India before that. I was as nervous as she was. On our second date, I took her to the Cairo Club, a nightclub where I had been once before with other friends, and she drank beer for the first time in her life. We enjoyed the evening together, and I enjoyed kissing a girl for the first time in my life. I don't know how I would have felt kissing a girl if I had taken the route of a traditional Hindu arranged marriage, where that first kiss doesn't happen until after you're married. But now I had a girlfriend!

I extended our relationship with a dinner visit to Ruth's parents' home and her church, and Ruth came to West Lafayette with me when I returned to Purdue. She was brave enough to sit down with me and her former boyfriend, who had introduced us, to discuss the uncomfortable situation we were in. He accepted the changed circumstances. We also visited the Risks, my foster family, and I introduced Ruth to them.

In 1962, Ruth was still working in Chicago, and I was still pursuing my graduate studies at Purdue. We continued to exchange visits between Chicago and West Lafayette and started talking seriously about marriage. I wrote to my family about Ruth and of our intention to get married.

This news understandably opened a Pandora's box. I was born into a conservative Hindu Brahmin family. They wanted me to come to India immediately, marry a Hindu girl—preferably from a family in our caste, as is traditional—and then return to America to continue my studies. Letters flew between me and my family members in India, Ruth and her family members in Chicago, and me and the Risk family in Lafayette. All the letters from India repeatedly emphasized the belief that the marriage between Ruth and me could not and should not happen. If it did, my family's name in India would be tarnished, and it would jeopardize the possibility of their making good marriage alliances for my two younger sisters and one younger brother. I told Ruth that I was also concerned about not ruining my siblings' lives.

Ruth's parents objected to the marriage as well. They were afraid that the mixed marriage would not only be a detriment to our living in the United States but would also negatively affect our future children's lives. They all recommended that Ruth visit India and study the situation before making up her mind.

My father, in Chennai, India, sent my oldest brother to America in December 1962 to persuade us not to marry. He repeated the argument that the mixed marriage would ruin the opportunities for our unmarried siblings. I could appreciate the situation that I had put my family in, but I was not convinced. Of course, I was deeply in love.

Ruth and I were both invited to spend Christmas with my American foster family, the Risks. However, just a few days before Christmas, they uninvited Ruth, not wanting to face any unpleasant situations that might arise with both Ruth and my brother being there at the same time. I had the unpleasant task of calling to tell her. She was understanding and went to San Antonio, Texas, to join her parents for the holidays instead. I was worried that it would be the end of our relationship, but we got back together later.

When my brother came to visit, he was not successful in changing my mind. I decided to go to India in the summer of 1963, when one of my sisters was getting married, and evaluate the situation. I warned Ruth that if I felt there really was the potential of hurting my family, we would have to postpone the marriage.

It was a difficult year for us. During my trip to India, I attended my sister's wedding and met most of my relatives. My closest relatives and friends all talked to me about the consequences of my marrying Ruth. But in all the conversations, the emphasis was more on urging me to marry a Hindu girl than on the negative impact if Ruth and I were to marry. By the time I returned to America after six weeks away, neither I nor my Indian family had changed our minds.

In 1964, major changes occurred in my career. I graduated from Purdue with a doctoral degree, and I received several offers of employment. I chose an academic position as an assistant professor in the Purdue School of Electrical Engineering. In sync with the professional changes, our social status also changed. In January, Ruth and I became engaged, and on June 6 we married in the Presbyterian church in West Lafayette.

My roots in America were growing deeper. In a mixed marriage where East met West, Ruth and I tried to bring unity in diversity to the wedding. Ruth's parents and two sisters, who are Baptists, accepted our marriage and participated in the wedding. Sadly, my father, and hence the whole family that he controlled, did not want to participate. But my foster parents, Kirby and Carolyn Risk, who are Presbyterians, graciously agreed to fulfill the role of my real parents.

A Lutheran minister who was associated with the local Wesleyan Foundation and was also a friend of mine conducted the wedding. My Hindu friend Mukundan was the ring bearer, and my Jewish friend Bob Elfant was the best man. Attendees were Purdue students, faculty members, and local friends. In addition to the Christian wedding, a small Hindu religious ceremony was performed by Mukundan and his wife, Hamsa.

Ruth and I spent our first Christmas with her family and all her relatives in San Antonio, and we were pleased that we were well accepted by the Pressler clan.

I had broken the conservative family traditions, but I wouldn't know until much later the larger significance of the changes. In one sense, my crossing the ocean and coming to America has become a model for my entire family. Several relatives in the second and third generations are now living abroad; most of them left their home country to pursue educational opportunities and subsequently settled outside of India. Several of them married non-Indian partners. One of my nephews, Mack, married a Japanese girl, Haruka, and they live in Tokyo. They had two weddings—a small Japanese one in Tokyo and an Indian-style one, with hundreds of guests, in Chennai. They are well accepted by both families.

But it was still hard in those first years. The two-way relationship and the communication between me and my family were temporarily frozen after our wedding. However, I continued to send financial support to my parents, and slowly we began to communicate again. Ruth and I had our first child, our son, Ravi, in 1967. Our daughter, Meera, was born three years later. I became a naturalized US citizen, thus establishing a permanent footprint in America.

Ruth and I felt that we needed to introduce our children to a religion that has no built-in dogma, and so we became members of the Unitarian Church, which is based on the "free and responsible search for truth and meaning." We raised our children emphasizing the guidelines of freedom and responsibility, and we encouraged them to choose any religion they wanted to when they grew up.

"Blood is thicker than water." In 1971, Ruth and I and both of our children visited my family in India. My two families—East and West—met each other for the first time, and it was a happy union. Ruth and the children adjusted to Indian customs quickly. I still remember the image of my mother feeding the grandchildren. It's a joint family, and so there were several children, including our eighteen-month-old, Meera. My mother sat on the floor with the children in front of her. She would take a handful of prepared rice from the pot in her lap and drop some in each child's outstretched hands, going from left to right. Then the children would feed themselves the rice. My mother would move on, from one to the next to the next, and repeat the process until the first course was finished. She was also talking to them in Tamil, her only language, telling them stories. The children in the group who spoke some English would do the translation. Then she would start on the second course. It was delightful to watch a bond being created between the generations and the families.

We have visited India with our children several times since then. With dozens of nephews and nieces to meet, as well as my parents and siblings to visit, we organize a PRM get-together (my father's name was P. R. Mahadevan). It has always been well attended. During our visit in 2019, my sister's grandson announced at the party that he was engaged to a Filipino girl, and there was huge applause. My sister humorously commented to me about the difference between my own wedding announcement in 1962—which was met with silence—and this one in 2019.

As I write this series of anecdotes of mine in the *Westminster Writers Journal* in 2023, Ruth and I have been happily married for fifty-nine years. I feel that I have established permanent roots in America and have left footprints, or dents, as I call them, in whatever I have been involved with. I think the Subramanian family is a microcosm of the modern family, building unity among diverse humanity.

* * *

I appreciate the assistance of Ruth and Meera, who reviewed the draft of my story and offered numerous helpful comments.

CASITA MORENO

Mary Lib Thornhill

It all began in 1948 when Papa came home from New Mexico and said that he had bought a piece of property on the eastern side of Wheeler Peak that overlooked Eagle Nest Lake, Baldy and Touch-Me-Not mountains, and Toby Peak. Mama and Papa had visited the Moreno Valley many times to pick me up from Cimarroncita Ranch Camp but had never owned property in that area.

I had graduated the year before from the University of Texas, and in the summer of 1948 I went to Europe; the trip was a graduation gift. While I was in Europe Mama and Papa visited the Moreno Valley once again, learned about the Idlewild Community, and purchased property there.

I wanted to ensure that our property had a clear view of the lake and the mountain peaks across the valley. Mrs. Cook owned the lots in front of those Papa had purchased and she was willing to sell them if, and only if, we bought all of her lots in Idlewild. They were not expensive, so we also bought her other lots.

Before I had even closed on the additional lots, we started building the cabin. Our builder lived in Angel Fire, New Mexico, and he did a fine job. There were two bedrooms, a kitchen, a large living room, and a deep porch facing the spectacular view.

During construction we stayed in a rented cabin at Laguna Vista in nearby Eagle Nest. Even before the cabin was completed, I took a train from Santa Fe to Mexico City and bought four chairs, a coffee table, a sofa, and a large, comfy chair to go by the fireplace. Then we all went to Trinidad, Colorado, to purchase additional furniture: a piano, a desk, and the bedroom sets. Papa bought several Navajo rugs which we still enjoy today.

Papa also bought a railroad light which would glow red or green. You could see the light all the way into town. Mama would face the green light toward town when they were at home so friends would know they were there.

In 1985, we added a bedroom and bath; we also converted a garage and laundry room into a studio apartment with a small living room, kitchenette, two bedrooms and a bathroom. The latest improvements include a new range, new siding, and a new table made from the old siding.

I have many memories of times spent at the cabin, our Casita Moreno. Here are a few:

A Bear Incident. Once, when my friends Susan Clevenger and Mopsy Burrows were visiting, Susan was startled by a bear peeking in her window. She asked Mopsy what to do, and Mopsy said, "Go ask Mary Lib." I came, and by then the bear was on the back porch digging through the garbage and tossing it everywhere. After the bear was off the porch, I banged garbage can lids together until he finally, finally, ran away. It took us a long time to clean up all that trash! The next year we glassed in the back porch so this would not happen again.

Taos. We thoroughly enjoyed our day trips to Taos to shop and dine. Between Bent Street and the Plaza is a boardwalk with shops on both sides that sell fabrics, leather goods, books, Indian jewelry, curios, furniture, and even ice cream. There is something for everyone, and the silver jewelry is to die for.

Often we ate at the Apple Tree restaurant. It was a charming spot. The food was delish, and sometimes there was a little combo playing. Other places we've enjoyed in Taos include Ogelvie's Bar overlooking the Plaza, the Overland Sheepskin Company, Taos Pueblo, the Rio Grande Gorge Bridge, the Leon Gaspard House, and the Nicolai Fechin House. There was an arts and crafts market on the south side of town. Many fine Taos artists—including founders of the Taos Art Colony—were represented there: Joseph H. Sharp, Oscar E. Berninghaus, Victor Higgins, John W. Lockwood, John Y. Hunter, and Bert Phillips.

Santa Fe. A trip to Santa Fe was always a fine excursion. Once we stayed with Mopsy's cousin, who had a beautiful home in Santa Fe. The restaurants are great, and the opera is a treat. We saw a performance of *Wuthering Heights* as the mist rolled in, which made it quite eerie. At one of the cafes in town, singers from the opera served meals and sang solos.

We sometimes went to the Indian Market; they spread their blankets along the north side of the Plaza and displayed their jewelry. Trips to Santa Fe wouldn't be complete without visiting its art galleries. The Fenn Gallery was my favorite. Northwest of Santa Fe, in Abiquiu, New Mexico, is Ghost Ranch home of artist Georgia O'Keeffe. Joan Hayden and I spent a week or so there painting Pedernal, a distinctive mesa that appears in various O'Keeffe canvases, and Abiquiu.

Tuesdays. Tuesday was bridge day. The players came to the community center in Eagle Nest from all over the valley. We usually started at Kaw-Lija's cafe for hamburgers, chocolate shakes, or delicious salads and ice creams, then on to the bridge game.

Vermejo Ranch. On Sundays, Jack Davis often invited us to have lunch with him at Vermejo Ranch, which had been bought by Ted Turner in 1996. The ranch had a large herd of buffalo that many visitors came to see. The lunch was always grand—steak, baked potatoes, veggies, apple pie and ice cream. Once when Mama and a friend were visiting, I took them for a picnic and to see the ranch. It was a beautiful day. We ran into Bessie Liedtki and her friends from Houston. Mama and her friend were exhausted, but we had a great day, seeing the deer and elk and the various buildings on the ranch.

Jaunts to Red River. Another favorite destination was Red River, a town about forty-five minutes northwest of Eagle Nest. It has many good restaurants, so about once a week we'd get a group together and go. We enjoyed wonderful steaks at Texas Reds, especially when there was a combo playing country music. North of the main street is a Mexican restaurant, and the Lodge serves fried chicken.

One day after eight of us had gone to Red River to celebrate a birthday, and several of us were returning from a hike, Jan Houser said she felt funny. She suddenly fell dead right in front of us!

Cimarron and East. Sometimes we would go to Cimarron, almost forty-five minutes east of Eagle Nest. We would stop there on the way to the cabin to get groceries and gear. The little market had a good selection of fresh meat, cold drinks, and paper goods—not as good as the Valley Market in Angel Fire, but it was on the way to our cabin. There is an old hotel, the St. James Hotel in Cimarron, that serves good Mexican food. Once, while eating there, we saw two llamas in the field across the street. The hotel was decorated with deer and elk heads, as well as bullet holes from Jessie James and Kit Carson.

When Mama and Papa were still alive and I was single, we would go to the races in Raton on Saturdays. Between Raton and Cimarron was Gretchen Sammis' Chase Ranch. She took me hunting and fishing. At Charlie Schreiner's ranch near Kerrville in the 1940s, I shot a deer. My trophy deer head hangs in the cabin; we call it "Charlie."

Once when Mama and Papa were visiting, I took them on a picnic in Vermejo to see the lodge. It was a sunny, beautiful day. We ran into my friend Bessie Liedtki and a good friend of hers from Houston. We saw many deer and elk —it was a great day.

Eagle Nest Tree Planting. One summer, Ann Knupp and I planned an Eagle Nest tree planting. We arranged it with Don Borgeson, the mayor of Eagle Nest. Irene Mutz, my next-door ranch neighbor, said we could have as many trees as we could use. So off we went with shovels and sacks to get the trees: firs, pines, and aspens. I think we planted about thirty trees that summer. We planted firs, spruce, and aspens in front of the Corner Market, in front of the Laguna Vista, and up and down the main street. We planted several more in front of the community center and in the park behind it. We had a truck with a large water tank that Moe Finley used to water all the trees we planted.

Hiking. We did a great deal of hiking. One destination was the Klondike Mine up the creek from the cabin. It was a producing silver mine for many years but had fallen into a state of disrepair and had become dangerous to enter. On one hike I did a painting of it from the roadway.

The summer I was sixty-five, we four friends, Theo, Jan, Elaine, and I hiked up Baldy Mountain. I had company, so we hoped we'd be back by five. We drove to Willow Creek and started up the mountain. They had hiking shoes, and I was in my comfy old boots. About noon, we stopped and ate sandwiches and cookies; Jan ate her sardines. When we got to the miners' hut, it was later than we thought it would be. There was a big discussion—which way up—I had been there with Papa and wanted to go left, but they thought we should go right. They all went right. I went left. I got to the top about twenty minutes before they did. What a view! To the east I could see Ute Park; to the south, down the Moreno Valley, were Cimarron and Angel Fire. We signed the log and headed down. It was getting cloudy, then dark, then rainy—heavy rain. Elaine had a yellow poncho, so she led the way. It was getting late, and we were soaked. All of a sudden, lights played on us. We jumped in a truck and learned we had been the subject of a search! When we got back to Theo's cabin, we were a mess and hungry. Quite a full day! I added a bead to the hiking necklace that hangs on my bedpost.

Irene. Irene Mutz enjoyed having me drive her around the mountains to see her property. On one trip to Red River, we were heading north from the highway and the jeep got stuck in the mud. So I hiked back to the highway, got a ride to her cousin's home in Red River, and came back with a tow truck. It was almost a whole day's experience. Another trip I took with Irene was up the road to Baldy Mountain. Our dog, Jacko, ran down toward the bog and got caught in the quicksand. I thought we had lost him, but he struggled out and came up, shaking mud all over us. We looked up the hill to the east, and there stood a huge grizzly bear on his hind legs, looking at us. Jacko chased over the rim of the hill, going after the bear. I thought, "That's the end of Jacko." But lo and behold, the bear turned on its heels and ran away!

Church. On Sunday mornings at 10:30, most of us went to church. The caretaker would have set out chairs. The outdoor service was very well attended. All the churchgoers introduce themselves and say where they are from and what church they belonged to and who was with them that day. The collection went to the general fund. Theo usually did the flowers, which were always beautiful. Jan Houser had donated the organ and often played. The choir, usually ten to twelve people, practiced on Wednesday nights. Sometimes we had a soloist—always a treat. A small cabin nearby sheltered the service when it rained. It was the site of the annual meeting, a Thursday game night, and once or twice, an art show.

Fourth of July. The Fourth of July was a festive day for all of us. Before the two o'clock parade down the middle of town, we would have a barbecue at the Eagle Nest Community Center. All of the proceeds went to the center. Idlewild had a rather large band led by Ron Wells, and it always won first place as the best entry in the parade. There were horses, wagons, floats, and jeeps decorated with flags and banners. One year, when the boys were young, Scoop put them and Jacko in the red wagon with flags on it. They were surprised to win the first prize for young entries. Everyone was delighted to post the blue ribbon on the bulletin board by the piano. After dark, the fireworks show started. It prompted a lot of oohs and aahs. Lots of folks from Idlewild brought their blankets up to the hill in front of our cabin to watch the show.

Lost Lake and Bear Point. Often we walked up to Lost Lake, just over the hill to the west. It was surrounded by aspens, spruce, and pine trees, with the wind always shaking the aspens. Sometimes Lost Lake held lots of water, and sometimes there was almost none, but it was always a treat to sit under the trees on the west side of the lake, watch the wind blow, and see the birds that come for a drink. Then we would go up to Bear Point and look over Eagle Nest Lake. Once on a trip up to Bear Point, we saw a bird's nest on the ground with three blue eggs in it. Of course, we covered it up a bit and hoped it was safe.

That Must Be the Place. One year the property was the location for a movie starring Sean Penn. The movie company arrived with a live buffalo, a stuffed buffalo, the actors, and the crew. The actors and crew all stayed in Red River. Mary Jane Parker came, and we stayed at the Laguna Vista during filming. Lucy and John Draper, from Santa Fe, also came for the shooting. We all were invited for the feast at the end of filming. It was supercalifagilistic—lobster, steak, veggies, and pie—the works. The whole thing was quite astounding.

For seventy-five years, my parents, my family, and my children's families have loved their summer visits to the cabin. Casita Moreno has been full of happy memories for all of these many years.

TREES

Mary Lynn Woodall

When I was five, my mother would read to me at bedtime. Some of my favorites were *Little Lulu* comic books. I loved the simple stories and pictures, while my mother laughed at the wry humor (which I never got). This was a time I remember with great pleasure. I also remember my wonderment that Little Lulu could walk out of her house and into the woods where she would often meet Witch Hazel. Looking back, I was amazed not that an innocent little girl could meet a witch without being frightened, but that she could just walk out of her house and directly into the woods. This was because we lived in El Paso, a city in the desert, where the nearest wooded area was at least one hundred miles away. If a tree grew in El Paso, it was because it was strategically planted there and watered with care. We had one large Arizona ash in our front yard that provided shade and respite from the summer heat.

But when I was ten, we moved to the big house on the corner which was surrounded by several large mulberry trees. One of those trees grew so close to our breakfast nook window that we could look directly into its spreading branches. We would often see the sparrows that came to rest there, but one day we noticed a hummingbird building a nest just outside the window. Each day we would watch her progress as she fashioned an exquisite little basket where she soon laid her eggs. It wasn't long before we saw tiny beaks appearing over the edge of the nest, and then we continued watching the mother bird as she tirelessly brought food for her young. I must have been at school when the babies fledged, but I was always grateful to have witnessed that miracle of nature. Another one of the mulberry trees was in our backyard. I desperately wanted to climb it, and I soon realized that I could do that by going up some steps to where a branch hung low enough to grant me access into its welcoming arms. I remember reading *Gone with the Wind* in that tree one summer. Although I wanted to stay there for hours, finding a comfortable spot to nestle in was a challenge.

Years later, after my husband finished graduate school in Fort Worth, we moved to Austin. I was ecstatic, for I was finally among trees again. Unfortunately, our first home, a rented house with a backyard surrounded by a chain-link fence, had only a small twig of tree in the backyard. Two years later, we decided to look for a house to buy. With the help of a very kind and patient realtor, we found a cute little red house for sale by owner. Our realtor arranged for us to take a look inside, but as I walked into the house, I was drawn toward a bank of windows in the living room which looked into a backyard full of native elms. While I stood there in awe, I saw a cardinal, a blue jay, and a woodpecker, and I knew immediately that this was where I wanted to live and raise my family. The flaws inside the house, like the painted linoleum kitchen floor and the lack of central air and heat, did not matter. I finally had my trees.

Over the next forty-six years, the house and yard saw numerous improvements and additions, such as a large deck and pergola where many dinners and other gatherings took place. Wonderful memories were made with friends who came to celebrate special events or just spend time together. And throughout all those years, the trees continued to grow and provide glorious shade and comfort, bearing witness to the love that was there.

Eventually, the house grew quiet and empty, and it was time to leave. The house went away, and sadly, the trees did too. But the memories that were created there have never left, and the gratitude and appreciation for those beautiful trees will always be a part of me. For it was those stately elms that called me to live in that space that day so many years ago.

Now, looking back, I smile to think that just as Little Lulu would walk out her front door and into the woods to meet up with Witch Hazel, I would walk out my back door into my own private forest where I spent many hours visiting with Mother Nature.

WORLD WAR II REMINISCENCES

Paul Youngdale

Where was I on December 7, 1941? Well, I was four years old, playing in the backyard of our home at 4308 Shoalwood Boulevard in Austin, Texas, with my older sister Ann. I'm sure some of the neighborhood kids were there with us. I remember Mother and Daddy lying across their bed in a back room with the window open listening to the radio and telling us to "Keep it down," so they could hear the news. That is all I remember of the "date that shall live in infamy"!

However, that day brought big changes in the life of my family.

My father was in the Army Reserves, having been commissioned as a second lieutenant upon graduation from Iowa State in 1932. He was called to active duty in March 1942, and after some training was stationed at Camp Barkeley near Abilene, Texas. Although he had been commissioned as an Artillery officer, he was assigned to the Quartermaster Corps because of his civilian occupation in the dairy business. He was attached to the Eighth Service Command, which provided housekeeping services to the Army installations in the south-central United States.

The rest of the family moved to Abilene in August 1942, as soon as Mother could travel after the birth of my younger brother, Ralph. We lived in several rent houses in Abilene during our three-year stay there. My folks were always looking for a house that better suited our needs.

The first house we lived in while in Abilene was on South Eleventh Street. Ann started the third grade in Alta Vista Elementary School that fall, and the next year I started the first grade there. For Ann and me, the days were filled with outdoor play, weather permitting. Most of the games involved playing "War." I remember during summer playing in the yard with hoses. The water brought wasps and yellow jackets in abundance. We attached nozzles to the ends of the hoses and used them to shoot down the critters. The yellow jackets were Japanese Zeroes, and the wasps were Japanese, or German, bombers. What fun! I don't remember anyone getting stung during these escapades. But, if they did, it was just a part of the game.

Another activity that we participated in was the collection of scrap metal and wastepaper. Periodically the city would announce a wastepaper and scrap-metal drive. That would occasion a frenzy of trying to have the largest collection of paper and metal on collection day. There was a dry creek nearby, and we scoured the creek bed for cans and other assorted pieces of metal. One kid found the top of an old car wedged between two trees. He won!

Another activity that Ann and I participated in was searching for enemy spies in the neighborhood. Behind our house was a large field, all mesquite trees and cactus. We spent many quiet hours lying on our beds and watching that field for any movement that might suggest the presence of spies. I'm sure Mother was happy to have us quiet for a while.

One vivid memory that I have concerns the pilots who were training at the Army Air Corps station that was attached to Camp Barkeley.

Mother had sent me to the grocery store a couple of blocks away to buy a loaf of bread. On the way home I was buzzed, at treetop level, by one of the student pilots. It scared the living hell out of me! I dropped the bread and took off for home as fast as my five- or six-year-old legs could carry me. I ran into the house, down the hall, into my bedroom, and under the bed! Mother coaxed me out from under the bed and went with me down the street to retrieve the bread. Along the way we also recovered a shoe that I had lost in flight. Not long after that, one of the student pilots crashed into a garage apartment a block or so from the school that Ann and I attended. I recovered a small piece of the plane from the wreckage and kept it for many years in my top drawer. I wonder whatever became of it.

Another memory of World War II concerns the German prisoners of war that were interned at Camp Barkeley. I assume that they were captured during the North African Campaign and brought to the United States because it was cheaper to provide for them here than in North Africa. For whatever reason, there was a large contingent of them at Barkeley. Some of them worked for my dad when he managed the commissary and the bakery facilities there. The first weekend the

Germans were at Barkeley, many people in Abilene came out to the camp and drove by the POW compound to get their first in-person look at the enemy.

The next day at work all the POWs could talk about was the line of cars that circled the compound. Two things amazed the POWs. The first was that civilians were allowed on a military base and the second, and most amazing to them, was the fact that civilians were able to obtain the necessary gasoline to take a Sunday drive!

My last memory of the war was V-J Day. During the summer of 1945, we had moved to Cockrell Hill, Texas, where my dad was stationed at the Eighth Service Command Headquarters in downtown Dallas. The word of Japanese surrender came after we kids were in bed. But Mother, who remembered Armistice Day as a child in Oklahoma City, prevailed on my dad to get us up and take us to downtown Dallas. We did not go all the way to the main streets of Dallas where the real celebration was in full swing, but we got within about two blocks and, looking down a cross street, we could see and hear the celebration. The street was a solid mass of happy people screaming their hearts out, horns honking and church bells ringing. What a happy night! The War was over, and Daddy had not been harmed. Hell, he had hardly gotten out of Texas!

FICTION

THE CLASSROOM

Lori Humphreys

That summer, Neddie Warren, Tommy Chen, and I spent nearly every day together. Though we attended different schools—Neddie, a private school; Tommy, the public school; and me, the Catholic elementary school—we knew each other because all the kids in the neighborhood knew one another. Our parents were friends, also. But, why or how that summer we became "us," I don't remember. Sometimes there is a magic to friendship; it just occurs.

Our rituals included blistering hop-scotch competitions, hiking down the hill to the park along the creek, and sucking orange popsicles while playing canasta in the afternoon heat. There was the discovery of our neighborhood secrets: the large empty field in the center of the block; the dairy-cow barn reincarnated as a multi -car garage; the mint chewy candies that the almost-blind man sold at the post office at the end of the block; and the horse chestnut tree that every autumn offered the neighborhood kids a bounty of shiny buckeyes.

There were few fences between the yards, and we could explore from yard to yard, sometimes filching the strawberries and raspberries that Mr. Guido grew. After dinner we graciously joined Jacob Eisenberg, Mary McGlone, William Lenzi, and our siblings to play hide-and-seek before darkness sent us home. We were old enough to relish our special companionship, young enough to be fascinated by our neighborhood's places and people, and innocent of the world that existed beyond its boundaries.

Mr. Krol, the local trash collector, was first on our list of fascinations. His arrival every Monday morning driving his horse-drawn wagon up my family's driveway to remove our accumulated trash was a hallowed diversion. We would sit in our backyard on the grass at the driveway's edge to await his arrival. Neddie would station himself at the end of the driveway and yell, "He's coming." And then run back to join us. Our heads turned in unison as Mr. Krol came into view, sitting on the raised seat of a gray, splintered, oak wagon urging Bessie, a brown horse, along with a graceful flick of his whip, and saying, "Up, up, Bessie." In unison we stood up and gazed with awe as they pulled into the drive. We shared an unspoken wish. Oh, to be on that wagon seat, flicking a long whip and saying, "Up, up, Bessie."

We argued about Bessie's merits, though whether she had any beyond the strength to pull the cart might be suggested by her commonplace name. But then everything about Bessie and the wagon was romantic to me. Once I asked, hesitantly, if I could sit on the wagon seat. Mr. Krol turned his expressionless face toward me and said, "No" and other indistinguishable words. His voice sounded hoarse and garbled, not by age, but from what I would learn was a foreign accent.

We watched Mr. Krol's majestic descent from his wagon seat. He was not young, but not old; strong but thin; dressed in gray; hatless. He nodded at us, and we nodded in return. He was a mystery we could only observe, not solve.

"Now, now, out of the cans," he would say, preempting any possibility of our obstructing his task of dragging the trash cans from their space behind the garage that was camouflaged by a fence covered in morning glory vines. With a single, magnificent sweep he would throw the refuse onto the back of the wagon and lower the can. When all the cans were empty, he would return them to their morning glory haven. Then my mother, with unerring timing, would come out, the screen door slamming behind her. She would speak with Mr. Krol and hand him a white envelope.

Neddie asked him once if we could buy Bessie and the wagon. Mr. Krol just looked at him. He did feed Bessie the apples that we had sneaked from our kitchens. More satisfying, he allowed us—marching soldier fashion—to escort Bessie and the wagon with him atop, down the driveway to the street. We would then watch, silently, as driver, horse, and wagon disappeared around the corner to collect refuse from other homes in the neighborhood.

Then, various bells and whistles began to sound, indicating lunchtime. That summer our mothers chose different signals to call us home. Twice a day, before lunch and after dinner, a neighborhood concert of differing bell tones and whistle pitches would tease our summer somnolence.

One Monday morning, Mr. Krol didn't appear. We were at our usual spot. Neddie went down the drive several times "just to check," he said. Mr. Krol didn't arrive.

"My mother will know!" I said. We rushed in to ask her why Mr. Krol had not come.

"Oh, something new is going to collect the trash now. The city has big orange trucks to do the job. It's much more sanitary," she explained.

"Also, Daddy will put the cans out this evening before tomorrow's pickup. "Might be something you can do, Bobby," Mommy said, looking at my young brother expectantly. He didn't look excited about that possibility.

The city was a distant, arbitrary power, and the decision made little sense to us. Big orange, mechanized trucks were not as interesting as Mr. Krol and Bessie.

My brother asked, "Will the drivers have whips?"

Neddie answered in his leader-of-the-people way, "Truck drivers don't need whips."

Tuesday morning, we stationed ourselves on our front-porch steps to get a closer view of what would happen. A big, orange truck with "SANITATION" written in huge black letters on the side made its slow parade down the street, stopping to pick up the garbage cans and trash barrels that my dad and all the other neighborhood dads had dragged to the curb the night before. We watched intently as it stopped in front of our house, the engine running. Two men jumped from either side of the back of the truck, with easy strength, and yes, something of athletic grace, lifted the cans and barrels up, emptied them, and left them upside down beside the curb. The workers returned mechanically to their positions, the driver shifted gears, engaged the engine, and the truck moved to the next stop, where the act of collecting garbage and refuse was repeated. We watched, silently, as the orange garbage truck made its way slowly down the street, like some strange, cautious beast, until it disappeared around the corner.

Mom came out. "OK, help me put the cans and barrels back."

After we stowed the cans and barrels behind their morning glory curtain, we returned to sit on the front-porch steps. We had no plans. Neddie asked, "Want to see the top of our garage?"

The Warrens had a garage with a second floor, and Tommy and I had pestered Neddie to see it. He said there was nothing there, but we were not so sure.

The chance to find out extinguished any interest in discussing the merits of orange garbage trucks vs. Mr. Krol and Bessie.

We did not speak of Mr. Krol. It was as though when he turned onto the road from our driveway that previous Monday morning, the future had swallowed him. The pattern of our lives continued, though the shadows of the elm trees spread across the lawns earlier each afternoon as twilight became darkness, and we played fewer after-supper hide-and-seek games.

A week before school started Neddie, Tommy, and I were walking up from the park. We had almost reached my home when I noticed two street cleaners who were pushing silt and sand that had accumulated at the road edges, into piles that would be picked up later by a vacuum machine. I was astonished to recognize Mr. Krol. He was looking down, concentrating on pushing the dirt ahead of him. His clothes were faded, and sweat stained the underarms of his gray shirt. He looked up and nodded at us. I didn't want to nod back. This was a stranger. This was not the man whose appearance had enchanted us a few short weeks ago. The three of us nodded reluctantly.

Together we stood and watched Mr. Krol as he and his partner moved on down the street. In an undeclared agreement, we never spoke of him again. School began, and though we remained friends, the three of us never again spent as much time together as we did that summer. The boundaries of our lives were changing— broadening in some ways, narrowing in others.

At the end of eighth grade, just as summer began, Tommy announced that his family would be moving to Kentucky in the fall. He would attend a high school in the northern part of the state. Tommy asked Neddie and me to drive up with him the September he began his freshman year, before his family left the neighborhood. Mr. Chen drove the three of us in a station wagon loaded with Tommy's stuff. I wondered, even then, what Mr. Chen thought about our chatter in the back seat. He didn't say much, but stopped to buy Neddie and me ice-cream cones on the way home.

Tommy would visit Neddie every spring vacation during high school, and we would reunite at my house or at Neddie's. Though I could not have known it, our senior year in high school was the last time we three were together. Neddie telephoned.

"Tommy is here. Want us to come over?"

"Of course. You can help me select my senior class picture."

When I opened our front door, they were there, smiling. I smiled. We were "us" again. Except now we were old enough to know that our childhood was over; young enough to believe in always; and not as innocent of the world that existed beyond our neighborhood.

VILLAGE WITHOUT MEN

The Second Journal of Anna Sophie Franziska Guenther
(continued)

Janice Shefelman

The story so far:

> When the War Between the States began, the highly educated German immigrants living in Comfort, Texas, declared themselves Unionists. Thus they were persecuted. Men were hanged and cabins burned. Now all able-bodied men have left to fight, on one side or the other, including Sophie's papa and her true love, Eduard. So the women must not only protect themselves from vigilantes and hostile Indians, they must continue to feed and educate their children.

* * *

Friday
June 3, 1864

School is over for the summer. We finished reading *The Odyssey,* and all I can say is that I am happy Odysseus found his way home to Penelope at last. After twenty years she did not recognize him in his beggar's clothing, nor did her suitors, who were drinking and feasting in his hall.

Penelope had finally decided that Odysseus would never return, so she ordered a contest for that evening. She swore to marry whichever man among them could string her husband's great horn bow and shoot an arrow through the rings of twelve axes standing in a line. It thrilled me when the beggar proved himself by being the only man among them strong enough and skilled enough to do so. It was then that Penelope realized that the beggar was her Odysseus.

But did he really have to kill all her suitors, one hundred of them? If Mama had suitors, Papa would send them off but not *kill* them. I guess those were more violent times—or were they? In our war men have killed one another by the thousands. Sometimes I wonder if we will ever learn to live in peace.

I should not say *we* when I mean *men.* We women in Comfort curse the war as we wait for word from our men and wonder who will return and who will not.

Wednesday
June 29, 1864

I promised myself to write only about significant thoughts and happenings in this journal. And today one of those happened.

On Wednesdays mail and supplies arrive at Faltin's Mercantile, brought from San Antonio. Sometimes very little, sometimes more, depending on the blockade runners.

Mama sent me there with her reticule to buy coffee beans and see if we might have a letter from Papa. We have had no word from him since my birthday. It seemed like every woman in town was there or had sent someone, like Etta and me.

She greeted me at the door. "Sophie, want to go swimming this afternoon?"

That sounded very nice, since the day was already growing hot. There is a swimming hole on Cypress Creek where Eighth Street ends at the water's edge. Young children swim in their underclothes, but girls our age just wade in the creek.

"Sure. I'll bring Willie, too."

"*Gut!* Tell him to get ready for splashing." Then she held up a letter. "This came from Papa, so I have to run home. Mama will be so-o-o happy."

"I'm glad for you, Etta. I hope we have a letter, too."

"I think I saw something in your mailbox. Maybe it's from your husband! You know—E.M."

Some of the women who were sitting on the front gallery chuckled. How Etta loved to tease me about Eduard. It used to irritate me, but no more. Now I want everyone to know that he is my true love.

"I sure wish there were some boys around here to kiss," she went on.

I laughed, remembering how she had kicked mean old Thomas when he bullied me at school one day. "I thought you preferred to *kick* boys."

"Ha! It all depends on the boy, Sophie, as you know."

She turned, leaped off the gallery, arms flying, and ran down the path and out the gate. "See you this afternoon."

I remembered when Eduard kissed me goodbye and went off to war. No boy had ever kissed me. I was only thirteen and he fifteen, but it sealed my heart forever.

So now I hurried inside the store, eager to see if the letter was from Papa or Eduard. It was crowded with women buying coffee, gossiping, and reading their mail. *Frau* Faltin, a slim woman with dark hair parted in the middle and pulled back into a bun, motioned me to come to the post office window at the end of the room.

She smiled as she handed me the letter. "From your papa, I believe. Your mother will surely be happy."

Though I felt relieved to know Papa was alive, something sank inside me. There was nothing from Eduard.

"*Danke, Frau* Faltin." I hesitated for a moment, then asked, "Just one letter?"

She smiled. "Be thankful, Sophie. Some women got none."

"I hope you got one from your husband."

"Not this time, but I know he is safe in Germany."

How I wished that Papa and Eduard were somewhere safe too. Slipping the letter into Mama's reticule, I said goodbye and started for the door, thinking only how I yearned to hear from Eduard.

"Wait, Sophie," she called. "Did you not want coffee beans? We received a nice supply, but it will soon be gone."

"*Ach, ja,* the coffee."

Even though the letter begged to be opened, I waited in line at the counter where the Faltins' daughter was weighing the beans. Talk went on all around me, but I was inside my mind. All I could think about was the letter. Where was Papa? Maybe he had some news about Eduard. I longed to open the envelope and read the letter, but it was addressed to Mama.

After buying the coffee, I ran home. Mama was sitting on the front gallery with Lena in her lap while Willie drew a picture of a horse in the dirt with a stick. He was always drawing in the dirt because there was a shortage of paper.

"Just like Papa," I told him as I passed, waving the letter for Mama to see.

He grinned and followed me to the gallery.

Mama gasped. "Oh, Sophie, let it be good news."

"Well, it means he is alive!"

My heart raced from running and anticipation. I handed her the letter and sat on the edge of the gallery with Willie.

Mama's hands shook as she carefully opened the envelope.

"Read it, read it," Willie said.

"Patience, Willie," Mama said. "I don't want to tear the envelope." Then she unfolded the letter and read.

New York
May 28, 1864

Meine Lieben!

I hope that you are well. Thank you for
your joint letter of February 14. I was
glad to hear that Sophie is helping Emma
teach Willie and other children to read.
And I enjoyed Willie's drawing of Max.
All in all, the letter lifted my spirits.

Still, I worry about your living in a
village without men. Sophie, you must keep
the pistol handy and loaded as I taught
you and be the strong one.

You will all be relieved to know that
I am alive, which is more than I can say
for many poor soldiers on both sides. War
is unspeakably horrid, and I must draw it,
battle after battle, day after day.

Harper's Weekly recently sent me to

Spotsylvania in Virginia. The battles
there went on for two weeks and I am told
that 32,000 men died! It is insanity.

I do not know of Eduard's whereabouts
but hope for his safety—though there
is no such thing in war.

The only good news I have to write is
that Lincoln was nominated for a second
term. But if the Union does not win this
war soon, I doubt he will be elected.

I think of you, Elisabet, Sophie,
Willie, and *kleine* Lena every hour. If
only I could embrace and kiss you. As
soon as this war is over, I will return.

Yours,

Friedrich (Papa)

Mama shook her head. "Why doesn't he just come home now?"

I scarcely knew what to say or think about Papa's letter. It was a relief to know that he was alive but awful to hear about so many deaths.

"You know he can't come home, Mama. Think what just happened to the deserter. At least Papa is determined to return as soon as the war is over."

Mama frowned and replied, "That doesn't mean he *will*, Sophie!"

Willie crawled over to her, sat on his knees, and put his head in her lap. "*Bitte,* Mama, no fighting."

She ruffled his blond curls and smiled. *"Ja, mein Liebling."*

Mama was right. Papa might not come home. Sometimes I think if this war does not end soon, she will make good on her threat to return to Germany, even though Papa cannot. And then what would I do? Would I stay here or go with her?

Nothing more was said about Papa's letter, but I could not get it out of my mind. *Keep the pistol handy and loaded and be the strong one,* he said. He knew that Mama did not want to do either.

I remember that when Papa left to go to war he said, *"Fortis fortuna adiuvat."* Fortune favors the brave. Odysseus knew that, but what about Hector in

The Iliad? He was brave and he was slain. What am I to believe? The truth is, I have no choice. I must be brave—like *Tante* when those ruffians came to her door. I must think like a soldier's daughter.

That afternoon as Etta, Willie, and I walked down Eighth Street toward the creek, I heard other children laughing and shouting, and I longed to be so carefree. But I have always been a worrier. I worried about Papa when he was here because of his editorial cartoons for the *San Antonio Zeitung*, which sided with the North—even as Texas seceded from the Union. Now I worry about him and Eduard, somewhere in the midst of battles. Will there ever come a time of no worries?

"What did your papa have to say about the war?" I asked Etta. As our village pharmacist, he had joined the medical corps in the Confederate army—not because he was in favor of slavery but because it was the easier way. And probably a wiser way than Papa and Eduard took.

"I don't want to hear any more about the war!" Willie exclaimed.

"Then run ahead and wait for us on the bank," I told him.

As he scampered away, Etta continued. "He said the field hospitals are crowded and unbelievably filthy. If men don't die from wounds, they die from disease." She paused. "What about yours?"

"He said 32,000 men died fighting in only two weeks! He calls it insanity."

Etta shook her head. "I wonder if any men will be left after the war."

"*Ach,* let's stop talking about it, like Willie says. Sometimes I think he's wiser than me."

"*Ja,* let's go swim!" Etta shouted.

Together we ran to the banks of the creek. There sat Willie on the root of an ancient cypress tree in his drawers, ready to wade in.

"Come on, Sophie!"

For the moment I abandoned my worries about the war, along with my shoes and stockings. Etta and I each took one of Willie's hands and waded into the shallows. He squealed as he lowered himself up to his neck in the cool, clear water, which ran over my feet and drenched the hem of my dress.

"Look here, Willie," Etta said, letting go of his hand and splashing water on his face.

Then Willie and I splashed water on her. She laughed and splashed me until my dress was damp and cool on my skin. Finally we crawled out and sat on the roots, where Etta and I wrung out the hems of our skirts.

For that moment, thoughts of the war and Indians were washed away.

Friday
September 16, 1864

The rest of the summer passed peacefully, and school commenced early this month. *Tante* has Etta and me reading about the Italian Renaissance and Leonardo da Vinci and Michelangelo. The title page of the book has a drawing of Leonardo, with his piercing eyes and long gray beard. It is a relief to read about another time and place and forget about the war.

But last night we had a frightening reminder.

Now that our village has no men to protect us, hostile Indians grow bold. They have stolen horses and cattle and even some women and children from isolated farms north and west of here. Last night they came to Comfort.

I awoke to a high, screaming whinny coming from the direction of *Tante* Emma's house. Could it be Pegasus? I put on my slippers and stepped out onto the gallery. The full moon had risen.

NNNNN-hhhhh, NNNNN-hhhhh.

Ja, it was either Pegasus or *Tante*'s horse.

I leaped off the gallery and ran down the street. At the end of Main I stopped at the rock wall in terror. There, some twenty paces away, an Indian was putting a harness on Pegasus. Another sat nearby, astride a paint horse.

"Pegasus!" I yelled.

He tried to back away, rearing up. But the Indian pulled him down, and both turned to me.

Then I saw *Tante*'s slim figure in the moonlight. Wrapped in a robe, she stood outside her front door, pointing her pistol at them with both hands, waiting for a clear shot.

What to do? My heart hammered as I stood in my white nightdress, practically naked with nothing to defend myself, in spite of what Papa had written.

Then I remembered what Papa told me a long time ago. I shouted the Spanish word for "German" at the top of my lungs. *"ALEMÁN! . . . ALEMÁN!"*

If they were Comanche, they would know about the treaty with the Germans and leave us alone.

For a moment no one moved or made a sound. The full moon shone down on us as if we were statues. Pegasus looked like the white mustang that the Indians call Spirit Horse. No wonder they wanted him.

But they were not Comanche and Pegasus was not all they wanted.

Using him as a shield from *Tante*'s aim, the two started toward me!

Gott im Himmel! My heart leaped into pounding.

Tante raised her pistol to the sky and fired.

But they kept coming, coming to carry me away! To ravish me. My legs trembled and threatened to buckle. One word shouted in my head: *RUN!* I turned and ran, stumbling and then falling. Any minute I would feel rough hands clutching me. I scrambled up, gasping for breath, and looked back.

NNNNN-hhhhh. Pegasus reared and knocked his captor to the ground with his hooves. He lay stunned. Quickly the other Indian leaped from his horse, grabbed Pegasus's reins, and pulled him down. Then, flinging the wounded man over his horse, he mounted, swung his horse around, and galloped off toward Cypress Creek, pulling Pegasus along beside them as a shield.

Tante fired again.

"Pegasus!" I called. "Pegasus!"

He tried to turn back, but the Indian jerked on his reins.

Pegasus had saved me but could not save himself.

Tears streamed down my cheeks and I put my face in my hands and wept. It seemed that everyone and everything I loved—Papa, Eduard, our home, my horse —was being taken from me. Even my maidenhood had been threatened, perhaps my life. Oh, what was to become of us?

Tante ran to the rock wall, and I hurried to her. *"Ach, Liebchen,"* she said breathlessly. "I was afraid they were going to take you, too! What are you doing out here, almost naked and without a pistol? They could have carried you off if Pegasus hadn't kept them from it."

"I know. It was stupid of me. I'll never go anywhere again without Papa's pistol."

"Gut," she said.

I hesitated, then thought, *When Mama hears about this, she will be determined to go back to Germany as soon as possible, in spite of Papa.*

"Let's not tell Mama about the Indians threatening me," I said. "I'm afraid she will make us leave Comfort."

Tante studied me for a moment, she in her modest wrapper and I in my thin white nightdress. I shivered, more from fright than from the cool air.

"Your mother is a dear friend, and I cannot keep such a secret from her."

"Even if I promise never to do anything so foolish again?"

"Nein, Sophie. All the women in our village need to know what happened tonight. If those redskins are stealing our horses, they'll steal women and children too, as you saw. We need to be prepared. Every woman in Comfort needs to carry a gun at all times and know how to shoot it."

She paused, thinking, and then went on. "So I'll put up a notice in Faltin's in the morning for everyone to meet on Saturday at the schoolhouse at ten o'clock. Can you and Etta spread the news around the village as well?"

I nodded, while my mind tried to grasp the fact that Pegasus was gone. He was a gift from Papa for my tenth birthday, an Arabian bought in San Antonio. I would never have a horse like him again. He had carried me some ninety miles out to the Nueces River to find Papa when he was wounded while trying to escape to Mexico and join the Union army.

"Do you think I'll ever see Pegasus again?" I asked.

"Only a miracle could make that happen, Sophie." She paused. "I'm just grateful that they failed to take you, too."

I reached across the rock wall and hugged her. "Because of you and Pegasus."

Then she held me by the shoulders. "Now, run home, bar the door, and get in bed. Tomorrow you must tell Elisabet what happened."

Back home, I could not sleep for the longest time. My hands and knees hurt from falling in the street. And my mind whirled. Would Mama be angry with me? What would she say and do? Would Willie and Lena be scared?

* * *

Note: *Village without Men* will be published in Spring 2023 by Eakin Press.

It is a sequel to *Sophie's War,* which Westminster library now has available for checkout. We will publish installments of the sequel in future issues of the *Westminster Writers Journal.*

GEORGE, EMILY, AND THE WORLD OF ALZHEIMER'S

Max Sherman

One would think that two Baylor students who were very much in love and who, between them, took almost every English course possible would inhale Elizabeth Barrett Browning's tribute to love.

> How do I love thee? Let me count the ways.
> I love thee to the depth and breadth and height
> My soul can reach, when feeling out of sight
> For the ends of being and ideal grace.
> I love thee to the level of every day's
> Most quiet need, by sun and candlelight.
> I love thee freely, as men strive for right;
> I love thee purely, as they turn from praise.
> I love thee with the passion put to use
> In my old griefs, and with my childhood's faith.
> I love thee with a love I seemed to lose
> With my lost saints. I love thee with the breath,
> Smiles, tears of all my life; and, if God choose,
> I shall but love thee better after death.

(Browning, "Sonnets from the Portuguese," Number 43)

George and Emily may have loved "with the breath, smiles, tears, of all [their] life," but it would take six years to mature.

Is this a novel or an autobiography? After years of taking notes, keeping scraps of paper of jotted-down ideas—ideas from a book read or a movie seen or a friendly conversation, even a boring lecture—it all came together with an explosive argument, just this morning, and of all places in an elevator.

Emily announced that she was not going to this place again; the place was The Place where she has done Pilates for ten years, and where George, at her urging had done Pilates for almost eight years. He was furious. After his pushing, probably a big mistake, to arrive close to on time for her Group of Six session, she seemed to protest at every nudge to "hurry."

On the elevator going to their VW after her announcement that she was not "going to that place again," George exploded with a profusion of pent-up frustrations: "Don't ever say that again. We are going to keep exercising, working puzzles, reading books, seeing movies, doing everything possible to stay alive as long as we are alive."

So, as she did Pilates and as George walked their Scottie, all of those notes, ideas, and scraps of paper started to make sense. So, is this a novel or an autobiography? It is both. It is a "novography," part fiction, part imagination, and part deeply felt windows into life in the world of Alzheimer's.

For example, as George walked their Scottie, Olive, who is dying of bladder cancer, and waited for Emily, who is struggling with short-term memory loss, his explosive, "We are going to be alive as long as we are alive," came alive for him.

Olive, who struggles to pee, dashes after every squirrel. If a tree has a new baby squirrel, Olive is at the base, those Scottie ears perked up, that distinctive black head at full attention. She is fully alive and shows every sign of being fully alive until that bladder quits working.

The six seventy-plus-years-old women doing Pilates are fully alive, staying beautiful, and in great shape.

It would seem that God's in his heaven and all's right with the world, at least on this gorgeous summer morning when everything around George seems very much alive. Why then his explosion just to get her there on time? Something he had always done—be on time—to that extent it was his compulsion and not Emily's.

George's frustration and guilt combined into what for him was a Roman candle moment of realization that he loved Emily so much that he wanted them to be like Olive and strain with all of their might to squeeze every single second out of whatever "alive" time was left. George was not prepared to give up one laugh, one tear, one smile, or one grumpy "I'm not going to that place again." Not one!

It probably had been love at first sight as I saw her radiant smile at the jailhouse door. She was playing the old pump organ. I still kid her by telling her I saw her well-shaped ankles as she pumped air into the instrument, but actually it was her captivating smile that touched my heart and kept showing up in my thoughts and dreams. We had just met. She was there to accompany four friends who had a great quartet and sang religious songs for churches and special events. They were doing a favor for me and a few friends who conducted regular Sunday afternoon services at the county jail.

We did not meet again in any close encounter until she came to the same college I had entered two years earlier. That does not mean we did not see each other. At least, I saw her at various church and school events, even though we attended different high schools and different churches. Always. Always I could spot her in a crowd because she was always smiling, that same infectious smile I first saw in the jailhouse. And to think I almost lost her. Thinking of the possibility of losing her, I am reminded of a few lines from a poem of R. S. Thomas:

> I have seen the sun break through
> To illuminate a small field
> for a while, and gone my way
> and forgotten it. But that was the
> pearl of great price, the one field that had
> treasure in it. I realize now
> that I must give all that I have
> to possess it. . . .

(Thomas, "The Bright Field," l.1-8)

Much like the prodigal son, but more like the third son the Bible missed, I did not want just the security and safety of home or the glamor of the far land, I wanted both: security and glamor. I was confused by my inability to choose one or the other, whether to stay home or go to the marketplace: to choose Emily, who was the rock of all that I treasured, or to choose glamor, which I thought might be with some other who might be more experienced in lovemaking.

I may have been like Steve Jobs: "Jangling inside him were the contradictions of a counterculture rebel turned business entrepreneur, someone who wanted to believe that he had turned on and tuned in without having sold out and cashed in. . . ." (Walter Isaacson, *Steve Jobs*, pg. 451)

Throughout there was always someone who spoke to one value or the other: Shirley, an intellectual soulmate in high school, but never a lover; Ruth, in college, another intellectual soulmate, but not a lover; and always a few flirtations and what might be thought of as passionate dalliances, but probably only a prodigal son's yearning for the more glamorous/instant love life, full of sound and fury, but never signifying any deep commitment.

Emily was also an intellectual soulmate. We discussed so many movies, books, ideas, religious practices, feelings, but never thought of ourselves as lovers. It was not in our particular form of Southern Baptist upbringing to let go into that mystery called love. But, and it is a very big but, Emily and I overlapped throughout my soulmate slips and my dalliances.

We met at the county jail when she was no more than fifteen, and for the next year I never missed her infectious smile in any crowd. When she radiantly showed up at my college, I asked her out, probably to one of those foreign movies that became such a part of our lives. She was smart, and we both were taking courses from challenging and stimulating professors; I'm sure we discussed those courses (history, philosophy, and English, for sure). I even became a frequent user of the Carroll Library, where I would arrive and seek out the table where I knew Emily would be studying. This was an almost daily rendezvous, and rarely did I miss slipping into the back row of the Tidwell Bible Building to hear her practice on the organ. My roommate and I took her to the most elegant seafood restaurant in town to celebrate her eighteenth birthday. I squandered my summer earnings to show my love, but I was not the least bit able to tell her, "I love you." Neither of us had that freedom.

We also had fun: taking her to her first ice-skating rink, putting on her skates and having a firsthand (literally) look at those ankles that captivated me in the jail; picnicking at my favorite spot in my favorite park, a spot never shared with any other soulmate or "dalliancer." On several occasions we drove twenty miles to buy kolaches at a Czech bakery for the two of us to indulge in or to share with best friends. We walked the Central Quad on campus, and I recited the Spenser and Shakespeare sonnets I had memorized to impress her, sonnets I again recited at her sixtieth birthday for her and special friends.

> One day I wrote her name upon the strand,
> But came the waves and washed it away:
> Again I wrote it with a second hand,
> But came the tide, and made my pains his prey.
> "Vain man," said she, "that dost in vain assay,
> A mortal thing so to immortalize;
> For I myself shall like to this decay,
> And eke my name be wiped out likewise,"
> "Not so," (quod I) "let baser things devise
> To die in dust, but you shall live by fame:
> My verse your vertues rare shall eternize,
> And in the heavens write your glorious name:
> Where whenas death shall all the world subdue,
> Our love shall live, and later life renew."

(Spenser, "Sonnet 75")

> Let me not to the marriage of true minds
> Admit impediments. Love is not love
> Which alters when it alteration finds,
> Or bends with the remover to remove.
> O no! it is an ever-fixed mark
> That looks on tempests and is never shaken;
> It is the star to every wand'ring bark,

Whose worth's unknown, although his height be taken.
Love's not Time's fool, though rosy lips and cheeks
Within his bending sickle's compass come;
Love alters not with his brief hours and weeks,
But bears it out even to the edge of doom.
If this be error, and upon me prov'd,
I never writ, nor no man ever loved.

(Shakespeare, "Sonnet 116")

It is now hard to believe that we never embraced or stole a kiss. It was not in our DNA to make that commitment when we both were driven by our upbringing: get your education; don't let anything interfere, especially a love affair, and certainly not sex, which can really get you in trouble. We both had many friends that had plans and goals torpedoed by a dalliance that led to sex and babies! Our Southern Baptist upbringing might also have been a factor, but our observation of high school and college classmates with that same Southern Baptist DNA alerted us to the danger of going all the way, and a passionate kiss could be a dangerous beginning.

Emily was the only one that overlapped all of those years. She was the "pearl of great price" that I almost missed because I was afraid to choose one life over the other. It was not fear of choosing her, but fear of not knowing which life to choose. The miracle is that she actually had it all, but I was afraid to believe both lives could be so totally in one person.

The large painting on the wall of our apartment started with a totally white canvas laid on the backyard lawn of our first 800 square foot home. Our son was four and our daughter was two. We had a basset hound named Jeff. The canvas is now and always has been a portrait of our lives. We call it "The Happening." It has all the elements of love. The sheer pleasure of bare feet on canvas, dog footprints, a bare bottom, tricycles, juice can, plumber's friend, a totally white uncluttered canvas now splashed with the vivid colors of life. Life and love.

Now, after eight years in the mysterious world of Alzheimer's, how do George and Emily make love? Every day. Every morning. Every afternoon. Covid threw a monkey wrench into daily outings at favorite restaurants: Maudie's one day, iHop another, Julio's for breakfast, Austin Diner for breakfast or lunch, and La Patisserie in Pflugerville, a favorite of Emily's, and those accidental discoveries where we stopped to "just give it a try." So much fun.

As an accomplished piano and organ player, Emily not only had gorgeous legs, but she also had strong, sturdy legs. She walked the halls of the memory unit to keep tabs on her fellow residents. She walked in and out of so many restaurants. George and Emily regularly found parks where they could sit and watch children play and where they walked the grounds. Several months of Covid isolation became the thief that stole Emily's walking legs. If you don't use them, you lose them. She is now in a wheelchair. As I write, I wonder how many hundreds, maybe thousands, are now in a world of wheelchairs because of the culprit Covid.

So, how do we make love with her in a wheelchair and with her angel friend and helper Monique always there to move her from place to place? Let me tell you.

Our days start with a totally white canvas. As Monique selects stylish and colorful blouses and slacks from the closet she asks Emily, "Is this one okay?" Often it takes two or three of those "okays" for Emily to nod her head up and down or to say "Yes," always with a smile and an occasional laugh. After putting on Emily's colors and fixing an Emily-style hairdo, Monique says, "Let's go see George." Emily's head, tucked down to her chest, pops up with wide eyes and a smile. She often says, "Yes," followed by mumbled words. When her head is on her chest she is not sleeping, just paying attention.

Once a week Emily gets her hair shampooed and spiffed up. On one occasion Emily pointed to the lady under the dryer and said, "Permanent." Monique asked, "Do you want one?" To which Emily immediately said "Yes," followed by a full hour of shampoo, hair set, and time under the dryer. When it was over Emily smiled and said, "I like it." She beamed as she was rolled into George's apartment.

How do I love thee? Let me count the ways during this eighth year of Alzheimer's:

A tricycle becomes a wheelchair. It gets you to the party!

Bare feet and bare bottom on canvas: Emily always wears well-chosen ankle socks. Often she crosses her left leg over her right to put it closer to George, and George tells stories, holds her ankle, and laughs when Emily bends her big toe as if to say, "I love you, too."

Dog footprints: George's Shih Tzu, Zelda, sits in Emily's lap, and she and George pet Zelda's soft black fur.

A juice can is the piece of apple or peach pie George saved from his lunch.

The plumber's friend, used as the artists' brush in making the painting, becomes the versatile computer on George's desk: it plays polkas, études, Scott Joplin music, and symphonies, or brings up photos of children and friends. It brings laughs and smiles.

George and Emily did not give up one single lovemaking thing. Not one. If she is not ready to leave his apartment, she holds his thumb and won't let go. Being together, holding a thumb, stealing a kiss are great Alzheimer's substitutes for love in the olden days. It is love and life in vivid color.

A SHARED EXPERIENCE

Carole M. Sikes

Colin arrived early to meet the friends who joined him every Wednesday evening in the main dining room of his retirement home. Three of his late wife's friends had been especially supportive when his wife suddenly died two and a half years ago. They had formed the pleasant habit of dining together once a week. The dining hall was unusually busy for a Wednesday evening.

There he is, waiting for a table, thought Colin as he approached a row of chairs by the dining hall entrance. There was an empty seat next to a man about whom he had been curious. As a writer, Colin was naturally inquisitive but tried not to be intrusive. However, this time his curiosity was personal, not professional. Before taking the empty seat, he registered his name with the hostess for a table for four and then joined the others waiting to be seated.

He turned to the stranger and inquired, "Is this chair beside you reserved?"

"No, it's available," said the man, without actually looking up in Colin's direction.

Colin sat down and introduced himself to the stranger, expecting to engage in conversation. But there was no reciprocal introduction. All the residents and the staff at the Brackenridge Retirement Center were extremely pleasant and friendly. Most everyone was known by first name. Last names appeared in small print on name tags and were often difficult to read or pronounce. Someone had told Colin that this resident's name was John and that he was a relatively new arrival but already had a reputation for being unfriendly, if not rude. He never wore his name tag, although all residents were encouraged to do so.

The stranger was an attractive, rather stocky elderly man, always impeccably groomed and wearing a suit or a jacket with a tie. However, he seemed uninterested in even acknowledging the presence of others in the retirement center. This was fine. There were certainly other residents who chose to be reclusive rather than social. But Colin was intrigued and felt challenged to learn more about him. He had observed that a driver in a clean, late-model BMW picked the man up each morning of the business week and brought him back promptly at 5:30 p.m. for his evening meal. Always he sat alone at both breakfast and dinner, at a two-top table near the windows. Colin had never seen him with family or anyone else, not even on weekends. He was never seen in any of the public areas except when dining.

"The meals are really good here, aren't they?" said Colin, again turning to the stranger.

"Yes, very adequate," was the reply, delivered with no physical affect.

Colin tried another question. "Have you lived here at the Brackenridge long?"

"Less than a year." This time it was definitely an impatient answer from the stranger who didn't even turn his head in Colin's direction.

"Well, it takes a while to get oriented." Colin finally gave up when there was no rejoinder and never even any eye contact between them. He was relieved to see his lady friends approaching.

Colin always enjoyed regaling the ladies with his adventures, of which there had been many. Tonight, the dinner conversation began when it was mentioned that the Shriner Circus was coming to town. That provided a great segue for Colin to talk about the summer when he had traveled with the Dailey Bros. Circus.

Dailey Bros. was a five-ring circus when the better-known Ringling Bros. Circus had only three rings. Colin had been fourteen years old when an acquaintance in his homeroom at school invited him to fly to Canada and join him and his family on a forty-four-car circus train. Colin's classmate John had refused to go with his mother and new stepfather, Mr. McDonald, who was the owner of the circus, unless he could invite a friend to accompany him. After the boys' parents met and the plans were approved, Colin and John's summer adventure with the circus would begin.

Upon Colin's arrival in Canada to join the circus train, the boys met with Mr. McDonald and were told that everyone traveling in his circus had to work. Their job was to pack boxes marked "English Toffee and a Prize." Older boys were hired to sell the boxes during performances. Colin and John doubted that the toffee was English and agreed the prizes were probably worthless.

"Boys, you are welcome to watch the shows, but you must be ready to crawl under the stands after each matinee and evening performance to retrieve any discarded boxes and prizes that look like they could be used again."

Colin's eyes met John's, and both boys registered astonishment. This was the first but not the only shocking revelation about circus life for these boys. Nevertheless, the next morning both new and used boxes were packed for the day's performances.

Mr. and Mrs. McDonald and the boys traveled in the private railroad car that had originally belonged to the president of the Pennsylvania Railroad. It had an extravagant Victorian interior of walnut-paneled walls inlaid with gold. This elegant car was located well in front of what was called a "pie car," which offered food and alcoholic drinks for the *butchers* to buy after they had been paid each night for their labor. The name *butchers* referred to the men who did the essential, backbreaking work in the evening and again on the next morning when the heavy canvas tents were taken down, loaded into the railcar, transported to a different town, then unloaded and secured for performances at the new site. Mr. McDonald made cash payments each night to the butchers, but only after all equipment and animals in cages were loaded, the performers were aboard, and the train could move speedily to discourage any of these workers from deserting. The last car on the train, adjacent to the pie car, housed prostitutes to service the men each evening. This scheme kept essential workers without money and therefore needing to continue their work, day after day after day. It was another revelation for Colin and John.

The hard-core circus performers told the boys more circus stories, many of which may or may not have been true. An example of a questionable story was about a diminutive five-foot-tall employee whose job was to feed the animals. After he had gone missing, small human bones were found in the lion's cage.

Before the summer ended, Mr. McDonald told the boys that he expected them to return the next summer, but they must become performers. When pressed for choices, Colin reluctantly replied that he would study to be a tightrope walker. What McDonald heard, or wanted to hear, was "the trapeze act." The famous Flying Wallenda family was hired to teach the boys during whatever time they could find. Colin remembered the blisters on his hands. Even when successful in catching the trapeze bar, he was never able to hold on to it long enough to return to the high platform from which he had leapt. Instead, he would drop into the net below. Then his trainers urged him to climb to the platform at the top of the tent to try again and again. This resulted in the failure of McDonald's plans for the boys.

When the summer season in Canada ended, the McDonald family of three boarded the circus train once again, traveling to the Texas town of Gonzales, where the circus wintered while preparing for another season.   After the tents were patched and stored, the animals housed for the winter, and the performers and workers paid and dismissed for several months, the McDonalds' personal belongings were loaded into two cars that their ranch hands had driven to Gonzales.

Mr. McDonald turned to address his two trusted ranch employees.

"Abel, you are to drive my wife and son in the second car. José and I will be in the lead car. Under no circumstances are you to permit another car to come between our two cars on the highway."

It was a twenty-five-mile drive of terror.

Mrs. McDonald had seen her husband put a handgun on the floor under the passenger seat in the automobile that would be the lead car.   Only when the Highway Patrol joined the two McDonald cars did she reluctantly confess to her son riding beside her what was happening. Her husband had learned that a robbery was planned to relieve the circus owner of the considerable amount of cash that he had in his possession. It had been a lucrative circus season, so Mr. McDonald had requested an escort to the family's ranch home.

They arrived without incident. However, the stepfather and stepson never became comfortable with each other, and Mrs. McDonald sent her son to live with his grandmother in a small Texas town. He lived an isolated life until he became eighteen and left for college. Eager to be on his own, he became a bright, ambitious, and hardworking student.

Colin returned home to a loving family excited to learn about their son's adventures. He appreciated the experience and used his unique story of summering with a circus to great advantage. It astonished and delighted his school friends. He used it as an icebreaker with new friends at college. With it, he entertained a beautiful woman who became his wife.

Colin became a professor, teaching university students about the pleasure of reading and the joy of writing. Coincidentally, his companion of that one summer made a career that was also related to teaching. He founded a publishing company and produced educational materials that were particular to the problems of diagnosing and teaching young children with learning disabilities to read and write. Both were successful and celebrated, making substantial contributions in the field of education. However, unlike Colin, John was dismissive of others and had no interest in meaningful relationships until he became reunited with his boyhood friend at the Brackenridge Center. John had been reluctant, but Colin was understanding and persevering. Colin's patience and generosity with his time was finally rewarded with John's brief but deeply loyal friendship.

A MEETING WITH SPIRO AGNEW

Boyd Taylor

It was Gwen who found the advertisement in *The Bookseller*. She and Edwin had been hired about the same time. When Edwin was introduced to the McGruder University Head Librarian, Dr. Thelbert Lindsel, Lindy—as everyone called him behind his back—cautioned, "Don't expect a long-term career here. We'll pay you minimum wage. We'll give you five years of good training. You will be able to go back to wherever you came from with a first-class résumé." He stood. "Welcome to McGruder University Library."

Edwin's master's degree in library science from St. Marius University did not count for much in Boston, the Athens of America. It was the spring of 1999, and his five years would be up at the end of the summer. He hadn't yet begun looking for what he'd do next. He liked Boston, its convenience, all the colleges and students. But the libraries were flooded with like-minded applicants who had more impressive résumés than his. Gwen, who was on a similar five-year track, had half a dozen interviews scheduled on the West Coast. Edwin refused to follow suit. "Earthquake, fire, and flood all at once? No thank you. I prefer my disasters at least a week apart."

Early in the spring term, Lindy summoned them. "I have an assignment for you." He handed Gwen a copy of *The Bookseller*, a London book-trade magazine, and Edwin a copy of *Publishers Weekly*. Each was open to "Rare Books and Collections for Sale."

"I want you to find us a collection we can afford. It's been years since we even tried to buy anything. Find me something important."

"How?" Edwin asked. "The important collections are handled by private negotiations."

"I know, I know," Lindy said. "But there is a gem out there somewhere. After all, I found the Bolivar Collection, with a draft of the 'Jamaica Letter,' in a trade paper! Find me another Bolivar!"

"What's his problem?" Gwen wondered when they were alone.

"Recognition. I hear he's in a struggle with administration about making the librarian a faculty member, instead of staff."

"With tenure!"

"Bingo!"

Not long thereafter, Edwin and Gwen sat in their carrels, deep in the bowels of the library. Thin book-trade newspapers covered Gwen's desk. Edwin, his feet propped on his table, was reading a novel. "Look at this," Gwen said. She pointed to an ad in *The Bookseller*.

Edwin took it from her and read aloud: "Estate sale of private Swinburne collection. Contact Dorby Fortnum, Esq. Trustee, D33, 299 Berkeley Square, London W1J8BD United Kingdom."

He handed the paper back to her and returned to his book.

"Well?" she asked. "Is it worth exploring? You do remember Swinburne? Poet. English Victorian. Something about a nude banister ride with his boyfriend? Didn't you major in nineteenth-century English lit?" She sighed. "You're impossible. Say something. Should we pursue it or not?"

Edwin shrugged. "I'm not eager to help Lindy. But if you want to, sure, go ahead."

Two weeks later, Gwen held up an envelope. "It's from England."

"Save the stamp."

Gwen opened the envelope. "It's about the Swinburne Collection. Remember?"

"Vaguely."

Gwen continued: "It's said to be the third-largest Swinburne Collection in the world after those of the New York City Library and the University of Michigan Library."

" 'Said to be,' " Edwin repeated.

Gwen ignored him. "He wants to sell quickly, to pay estate taxes. He has approval from the Export Licensing Unit to sell the collection outside the UK." She handed Edwin the letter. "What do you think?"

Edwin scanned the letter. "It might be just our thing. The British government has said it's not worth keeping in Britain."

The next day Lindy visited their workstations for the first time. He held Gwen's summary in his hand. "I was hoping for something Latin. Swinburne? Really? Is this for us?"

Edwin glanced at Gwen, then said, "Perhaps not. It's in London. Someone would have to inspect it. Ideally, someone familiar with London and with Swinburne."

Lindy rubbed his chin. "That's true." After a minute, he said, "Well, I did do some of my doctoral research at King's College." He paused. "In London." The words came quickly now. "And as it happens, I have always had a strong interest in Swinburne. I considered doing my dissertation on the Pre-Raphaelites."

"Oh, you would be perfect, Dr. Lindsel," Gwen said. "Could you go over and examine the collection?"

Lindy said, "It would have to be quickly, before it gets away."

The next morning, Lindy stopped by to tell Gwen and Edwin the latest. "The provost approved my trip. Get me a copy of the *Sunday Times*. I want to see the theater listings. I wonder what's happening at Royal Albert Hall."

A few days later, Gwen answered her phone, and then nodded. "Yes. Have a safe trip home." She said, "It was Lindy. He wants us to prepare a presentation for the provost on Monday."

Provost Jeff Hardin's office had a large desk, covered with neatly arranged stacks of papers; the office also had enough space for a recliner and a conference table, where Lindy, Gwen, and Edwin waited while the provost signed papers. Edwin caught a glimpse of the sunlight on the reflecting pool in the quadrangle. A beautiful New England day. He whispered to Gwen, "He has windows!"

She frowned. "Shhh."

The provost soon joined them. "So, Lindy, what expensive scheme have you got this time? A new collection to add to your empire?"

"Jeff," Lindy said, "this is an opportunity for McGruder University Library to acquire one of the largest Swinburne Collections . . . "

The door opened and a voice—Mid-Atlantic meets Southwest, and familiar to all McGruder faculty and staff—said, "Jeff, this report . . . " It was McGruder University president Addison Freemont "Call me Monty" Rector. McGruder trustees had lured Monty to Boston to bring order to the university's chaotic finances and recalcitrant faculty. "Oh, sorry to interrupt. I'll catch you later."

The provost said, "That's okay, Monty. Lindy has a collection he wants us to buy. Swinburne."

Monty turned. "Swinburne? Now, that's interesting. May I join you?" He leaned across the table and shook hands with Gwen and Edwin. "Call me Monty." Edwin nudged Gwen. She stared straight ahead. Monty said, "Go on, Lindy. What's this about Swinburne?"

Lindy's hands trembled as he looked at his notes. "As I was saying, sir, . . ."

"Call me Monty."

"Uh, Monty, this is an opportunity to acquire one of the largest collections of Swinburne's papers."

"How major is it?" Monty asked.

Lindy cleared his throat. "Very. The manuscripts include poems, essays, fragments of plays, criticism, and handwritten notes toward works. Letters to and from Swinburne with Ford Madox Brown, Robert Browning, all the big names. Thousands of documents and paintings." He paused for breath. "I have examined the collection myself. It has been authenticated by a leading Swinburne scholar at King's College." He looked up. "Under whom I studied."

"That's good, Lindy. A fine job," Monty said. "How much do they want?"

Lindy said, "Probably two hundred thousand, maybe two fifty. Dollars."

Monty leaned back in his chair. "Jeff," he said to the provost, "did I tell you about my conversation with Mark Kill at the DC alumni dinner?"

The provost replied, "I recall you saying that you struck out."

"I was all set to pitch him a new IT building, but he didn't want to talk technology at all. He wanted to talk poetry."

"Poetry? Mark Kill is a poet?"

"Maybe. I don't know. I do know that he's obsessed with poetry." He paused and smiled. "Not only poetry, but nineteenth-century English poetry." He looked at the others, and smiled more broadly now. "And not only nineteenth-century English poetry, but . . ."

The provost gasped. "Seriously?"

"All our young tech billionaire alum wanted to talk about was Swinburne. Swinburne this, Swinburne that. I gave up."

"It was hopeless."

"Hopeless."

Monty turned to Lindy. "Lindy, didn't you propose a new wing to the Main Library?"

Lindy replied, "Last year. You shot it down."

Monty laughed "Jeff, get that proposal out. Hang 'Swinburne Collection' on the front of it. Name it the Mark Kill Wing. How much was it?"

"Ten million."

"Beef it up to fifteen. A new wing, featuring our Swinburne Collection. Buy the damn collection. I'll call Mark."

A few weeks later, Gwen and Edwin found themselves at the Mark Kill Conference Center outside Baltimore. Before they left Boston, Lindy cautioned them: "This is an exploratory meeting. The president will handle it all. You're technical support. Understand?"

The conference center was in a leafy area on the outskirts of Baltimore. They were greeted by a young woman, who said, "Be careful. Renovation is still going on."

"What is this place?" Monty asked.

"It has a troubled history," she answered. "Mr. Kill is making it a vibrant part of the community, better than it ever was."

They had arrived before Kill, and Lindy now dismissed them, saying, "Stay nearby."

They found an empty office where they could wait, and Gwen said, "We're ready, aren't we?"

Edwin replied, "I am if you are. I think I'll look around."

"You're no help at all."

"Fortunately, I have you."

"Go, go. I've got this."

Edwin's footsteps echoed in the unoccupied building. He came to a large central court surrounded by empty offices. The fountain in the middle of the court had been drained, doors were off their hinges, and light fixtures dangled where ceiling tiles had been removed.

A tall man in a black suit with a red tie stood amid the debris. He turned to Edwin, and said, "They're erasing all memory of me."

"I'm sorry. What did you say?"

The man extended his hand. "Who are you?"

He gripped Edwin's hand and did not release it until Edwin answered. "I am Edwin Roberts. Excuse me, sir. You look familiar. I think I should know who you are."

"That's all right. I'm just a face in the crowd now." He gestured at the debris. "When they are done here, no one will remember what this place once was."

" 'Once was?' "

"I dedicated it when it was built in 1969, just after President Nixon and I were elected. It was going to house my library, but political events intervened."

Edwin exclaimed, "You're Spiro Agnew!"

"Guilty as charged!" Agnew laughed. "I plead guilty to being me. Not to anything else. I never admitted any wrongdoing. I did have a plea deal, however. Why? you may ask. It's simple. The Justice Department and the State of Maryland had more lawyers than I could afford. I ran out of money. Otherwise I'd still be fighting them."

"That was Watergate?"

"Oh, heavens, no. I had nothing to do with that batch of bungling burglars. My trouble was that the establishment did not want Agnew to succeed to the presidency if Nixon was impeached. They wanted me out, so they decided that the way every Maryland governor had always done business was suddenly illegal. A political vendetta conducted by Nixon's hatchet man. Elliot Richardson, that lily-livered little liar. 'Go quietly. Or else,' he told me. And when I did resign, Nixon stood by and let the prosecutors come after me." He exhaled. "Oh, well, what's done is done." He took Edwin's arm. "Would you like to see my office? They haven't ripped it out yet."

Edwin hesitated. "I have a meeting."

Agnew replied, "There's plenty of time. You can hear Kill's helicopter ten minutes before it lands. Then he always has to make a pit stop." He smiled. "The kid must have a loose bladder. It happens every time he has a meeting here."

Agnew pulled down the yellow tape that was across the entrance to the office. "Come in. Have a look around. This is exactly like my office when I was VP."

Edwin stepped inside. Dusty volumes occupied a wall of bookshelves. He picked up a copy of *Atlas Shrugged* and flipped through it. It was filled with red notations, circled passages, and exclamation points.

"Do you know Ayn Rand?"

"Not really."

"You should. It can be life-changing."

Edwin smiled. "My life needs changing, but I don't think Ayn Rand has the answer."

Agnew took the seat behind the large walnut desk and said to Edwin, "Sit down, please."

Edwin brushed the dust off one of the leather chairs and sat, facing Agnew. "I have to say, I never expected to meet you here today."

Agnew leaned forward. "Why are you meeting with Mark Kill, Edwin?"

Edwin hesitated, then said, "I guess it's not a secret. I work in the library at McGruder University in Boston. I'm here because the university is seeking a grant from Kill's foundation to build a new wing on the library."

Agnew grimaced. "Ah, Boston. That isolated island of intellectual ignorance —the home of my friend Elliot Richardson."

"I like Boston, a lot."

"And you want Kill to give McGruder University the money?"

Edwin replied quickly. "I really don't care. My probationary period at McGruder is over, and they say there's no permanent position for me."

Agnew stared at him. "What do you really want, Edwin?"

Edwin thought for a moment, then said, "I don't know. I guess all I really want is to stay at McGruder."

Agnew laughed. "Stay? In the library? Is that all?"

"I'm not ambitious. But even that seems beyond me."

The sound of helicopter blades echoed through the empty halls. "There's the kid." They rose. Agnew put his arm around Edwin's shoulders. "A word of advice from a Greek immigrant's son, who was almost president: Don't let anyone deny you your dream. I did that, and I've regretted it the rest of my life."

Later, during the meeting with Kill, Gwen and Edwin listened as Monty described the Swinburne Collection. "It's the largest collection of Swinburne materials held in private hands. It's so good we bought it even though we don't have a place to display it."

Kill smiled. "So . . . you're using Swinburne to encourage me to get out my checkbook?"

"You know me too well, Mark," Monty said. "It's true. I remembered your interest in Swinburne. And the library needs a new wing. Are you interested?"

"I might be," Kill answered. "How much?"

"For the collection itself, under half a million. But we think it could be the centerpiece of a fifteen-million-dollar wing for the Main Library."

Kill stared at Monty, then said,

"Was life worth living then?
And now,
Is life worth sin?"

The room fell silent. Monty shook his head. He looked at Lindy, who gaped.

Kill repeated,

"Was life worth living then?
And now,
Is life worth sin?"

"Nothing?"

A moment passed, and then a voice came from the back of the room. It was Edwin.

"Where are the imperial years?
and how
Are you Faustine?

"We have a first draft of that." They turned and looked at him. "*Faustine*. We have *Faustine* in Swinburne's own hand, the first time he ever wrote those words."

"Who are you?" Kill asked.

"My name is Edwin Roberts. I work in the library."

"So, Edwin," Kill said, *"Before the beginning of years"*
Edwin answered,

> *"There came to the making of man.*
> *Time, with a gift of tears."*

"I don't suppose you have a first draft of that?"

"*Atalanta*? No. But we do have a first edition, given by Swinburne to Dante Gabriel Rossetti."

"Edwin, Edwin," Monty said. "Sit up here, beside me." Edwin could see that Monty had written his name, with a question mark on his notepad. The president motioned for Lindy to make room.

Kill said, "Tell me about the collection, Edwin."

For an hour, Edwin described the collection. He answered Kill's questions without hesitation. Monty watched. Once he motioned for Lindy to be silent when he tried to interrupt.

Finally, Kill stood, extended his hand to Edwin, and said, "It's a pleasure to meet someone so knowledgeable, who shares my love of Swinburne." Then he said, "I'll do it, Monty. Send the papers and the drawings to my people. Better still, have Edwin bring them. We have a lot to talk about. And of course, I want Edwin to be in charge of the Swinburne Collection."

"Naturally, Mark. After all, he's our Swinburne expert."

After Kill left, Monty took Edwin aside. "Come to my office tomorrow and we'll work out the arrangements. Meanwhile, why don't you and the young lady take a later flight? I have some work to do with Lindy."

As Gwen and Edwin waited outside the conference center for their taxi, Gwen frowned and said, "What a performance. How did you do it?"

"I have a very good memory—some say a photographic memory. And I did my thesis on Swinburne."

"You are a bastard. You never told me you were a Swinburne scholar! Why didn't you tell Lindy?"

"He would have appropriated anything I told him. He'd already given me my notice."

"I get that. But why not tell me?"

"I don't know. Maybe I just didn't want to get involved."

She shook her head. "Until today. You certainly got involved today. Why?"

Edwin smiled. "I was just following Spiro Agnew's advice. He told me to man up. And he was right."

They watched their taxi pull into the circular drive. Gwen said, "Just a minute. Spiro Agnew? The corrupt vice president?"

"He says he got a raw deal. I don't know if he did or not."

"You're taking career advice from Spiro Agnew?"

"Good advice can come from bad people." He opened the door for her. "And it worked." He grinned. "Swinburne Collection Librarian."

Gwen fastened her seat belt. "Wipe that smile off your face. And anyway, you liar, isn't Spiro Agnew dead?"

Edwin shook his head. "He's not dead. I talked to him before the meeting."

The driver was listening. "Agnew died three years ago. I drove some of his family to the funeral. Not many people there."

"See there? He's dead."

Edwin grunted. "I talked to Spiro Agnew."

"He's dead," Gwen said. "Was it a specter? An impersonator? An hallucination? Maybe you were channeling your inner Spiro?"

Edwin closed his eyes. ". . . Dead or alive, he gives good advice."

CONTRIBUTORS' NOTES

BARBARA ADAMS. I was born in San Antonio, Texas, and went to private and public schools there and Holton-Arms School, Washington, DC. I attended Mary Washington College in Virginia. I won two awards for oil painting in a national show in Washington, DC and illustrated a children's book, *On Gustavo's Farm,* written by my daughter's very special goose, Gustavo. Also, I have sculpted Father Christmas figures from clay which were then made into molds.

KEN ASHWORTH. I am a former vice-chancellor of UT System Administration and former Texas Commissioner of Higher Education. I also served on the adjunct faculty at LBJ School of Public Affairs at UT Austin and at The Bush School of Government and Public Service at Texas A&M.

ROBBIE AUSLEY. I grew up in Lubbock, Texas. I met my husband there at the Methodist Church where we were married 60 years ago. I put Tom through Texas Tech and then UT Law School. Austin became home and we raised our four children here. Over the years I have been active at First United Methodist Church, Austin, involved in Austin public schools and Planned Parenthood. The proud grandmother of ten, I enjoy tennis and travelling and am an avid walker, usually walking two miles a day.

MARY LEA BAKER. When I was growing up in the deep East Texas city of Longview, it never occurred to me that I would meet and marry Frank Baker, a soon to be newspaperman, and spend almost 50 years of my life in far West Texas. Together, with our staff, we published The Fort Stockton Pioneer twice weekly. As Life Style editor, I put my Interior Design degree from the UT school of Home Economics to good use. We were blessed with three children and three grandchildren. Also, I have smartest one-year-old great grandson ever! Frank passed away in 2019. I moved to Westminster in July, 2021, and have enjoyed meeting new friends.

BETSY BOUCHARD. I am a runaway Texan, having spent most of my life elsewhere, but I kept some roots. My Austin grandmother instilled a love of reading; my East Texas father, a love of words; my grandfather, a rocky piece of the Hill Country. In the '60's, when the university was the place to be, I took my time acquiring degrees, a husband, and finally a job in Chicago in the City Colleges, eventually returning to the family ranch and nearby family. Friends from first grade through high school have got back in touch. New friends at Westminster keep me on my toes and make returning to Austin a homecoming.

FLOYD BRANDT. Now entering my tenth decade, I am a retired professor of business. I taught approximately 7000 students on five continents, written poetry since my teens, and published several books before retiring. Since retiring to Westminster I have written ten unpublished but bound books.

LEXA CRANE. Yes, I am still writing. The door to my apartment has magnetic clips for thoughts and writing. Stop by Apartment 317 for a peek. People ask how I choose what to write. The answer is to look around. The curve of a tree trunk, splattered mud, or a crushed flower all entice me on my walk and I write.

SHIRLEY DEAN. Born in Ohio, I moved to North Carolina when I was a teen. I earned a BS in in nutrition from University of North Carolina Greensboro, and an MPH from the University of Michigan. I am also a Registered and Licensed Dietitian. I married Ernie Dean in 1955, and enjoyed twenty years as the wife of a career USAF officer. While he attended Austin Presbyterian Seminary, I spent those three years auditing classes and twenty-five more years as wife of an ordained minister. I retired after thirteen years as a member of the biology faculty at Texas Lutheran University. Writing has always been my way of expressing thoughts, clarifying issues, working through problems and treasuring memories.

LORI HUMPHREYS. As a co-managing editor I enjoy encouraging neighbors to write for the *Westminster Writers Journal*. It is satisfying and safer than putting yourself out there with a poem, essay, memoir or short story. But I have been thinking I would like to try my hand at fiction and chose to do just that in this issue. It's scary being out on a limb, but it is exhilarating!

MARY KEVORKIAN. I grew up in Michigan and attended the University of Michigan in Ann Arbor. I received my master's degree from USC and taught public school music and piano. I came to Texas in 2000.

PAUL R. LEHMAN. I am a professor emeritus at the University of Michigan. Until my retirement I was the senior associate dean for the School of Music, Theatre & Dance at Michigan. I am a past president of the 130,000 -member National Association for Music Education, a member of the Music Educators Hall of Fame and an honorary life member of the International Society for Music. My eyesight is not very good, my hearing no better, and sometimes I can scarcely remember my name. But I still have my driver license.

RUTH LEHMAN. As a French horn player, I have performed in symphony orchestras in Canton, OH; Boulder, CO; Lexington, KY; Brockport, Penfield, and Greece, NY; and Ann Arbor, MI. My husband Paul and I have given 80 presentations at Westminster and have taught courses for SAGE, QUEST, and FORUM, at UT OLLI. I have a Bachelor of Business Administration degree from the University of Michigan.

BEN LINDFORS. I taught English and History at a boy's boarding school in Kenya from 1961-1963. When I returned to the U.S., I entered a doctoral program in English and African Studies at UCLA. In 1969 I joined the faculty in the English Department at UT where I taught courses in African literature and culture for the next 33 years.

KATHERINE McINTYRE. I grew up in Massachusetts. My husband, Bernie, and I married after meeting at Northeastern University in Boston. We have lived in New York and Texas. I worked raising children and writing software for Lockheed Martin and spent ten years in local politics as a city council member and mayor of Clear Lake Shores. We have three sons and seven grandchildren.

TRACY NOVINGER. I was born in Aruba, lived in Brazil where I attended local schools and graduated from the University of Colorado and have an MA in communication. I moved to Tahiti for nine years and was a French-English interpreter for the courts. I speak fluent English, Portuguese, French and Spanish, elementary German and Italian. I met my husband, Glen, in the US. Currently I am working on my fourth novel, set in Tahiti. I have published three books.

THEO PAINTER. I am a native Austinite, a graduate of Austin High School, UT Austin and UT Medical Branch, Galveston. I had a private practice as an Allergist for over 50 years. My wife, Dorothy Buckley, an Oklahoma native, and I have two daughters and one son. My favorite pastimes include carving birds from wood, hunting and spending time on the Texas gulf coast.

RANDY PARKER. I grew up in Madison, WI, and obtained a PhD in psychology from the University of Missouri in Columbia. I was a professor at the UT Austin from 1969 until retiring in 2012. I am a professor emeritus in special education and was a licensed psychologist for 45 years. My late wife, Donna, and I had three daughters and seven grandchildren. Donna passed away in 2018 from Alzheimer's. I was surprised by joy when I renewed acquaintance with Barbara Adams, and we married in June 2021.

THEODORE REUTZ. Having failed to reach South America at age 18, I then hitchhiked sixteen times between Little Rock and college in Philadelphia, hitchhiked to the Central University of Venezuela, and subsequently through the jungle and on DC-3s to Rio de Janeiro, returning for an MA at Stanford.

MIKE ROCHE. I am a lifetime resident of Austin and a 1957 graduate of UT Austin. My career was in financial services. I am married to Gayle and we are the parents of four children and have six grandchildren. I enjoy hunting, reading, and collecting toy soldiers. We retired to Westminster in late 2015.

SAM SAMPSON. While seminary was essential in preparing me for ministry, my intern year at the Caltech Y made a unique contribution. It helped me get a position as a campus pastor, and had a great influence not only on those 13 years, but on my entire ministry. My intellectual development, ethical concerns, and ministering to people in a variety of different ways have been shaped by that year. My political views, concern for climate change, and my support for feminist convictions on the equality of women, owe a lot to my year at Caltech.

PHYLLIS SCHENKKAN. My academic training was in both theatre and English. I have worked as a costumer and as a high school English teacher with some other activities thrown in. Austin has been my home since 1956.

WILLIAM SCHLEUSE. I grew up in Austin and San Antonio and am a graduate of UT Austin and the UT Medical Branch in Galveston. I practiced and taught psychiatry and psychoanalysis in Houston and Austin for more than forty years. I've also enjoyed sailing, flying, photography, travel, and in recent years, studying and teaching the history of photography, which has led me into history.

JANICE SHEFELMAN. I am the author of award-winning books that bring the past alive for children and adults. My husband, artist and architect Tom Shefelman, illustrated them. I grew up in a university neighborhood in Dallas, where my professor father read to me when I was a young girl. Thus began a love affair with books, which led to my careers as teacher, librarian, world traveler, and writer.

MAX SHERMAN. My wife, Gene Alice, and I moved to Westminster in April, 2012. She is now in Memory Care. This is an important part of our lives.

CAROLE M. SIKES. I was born in 1934 and married in 1958. My education includes a BFA from UT Austin, 1956; graduate study, Columbia University Teachers College, New York, 1957; and an MFA from UT Austin, in painting and printmaking, 1965. I taught in San Antonio public schools and at the Austin Museum School of Art. I am represented in the Archives of Women of the Southwest, SMU DeGolyer Library. My art has been in group shows and three solo exhibits. My published books are: *Fairy Tales Are Real* (Plain View Press, Austin) and *Hudson Bend and the Birth of Lake Travis* (History Press, Charleston, SC).

JUDY SKAGGS. I grew up in Eldorado, Texas, a small -2400 population on a good day- West Texas town where my four grandparents lived. Talk about being spoiled! I attended North Texas State University and graduated from the University of Houston with a degree in Education. My teaching career was one semester. When I moved to Austin, I was church organist at Covenant Presbyterian Church for 20 years. When my four children were raised, I graduated from Austin Presbyterian Theological Seminary and was privileged to serve several Presbyterian churches in the Austin area. I have six grandchildren (two are married) and one great-granddaughter. I love living at Westminster, visiting with friends, reading and always playing music.

JOAN SMITH. I grew up in China and continued school in North India and the United States. I taught elementary school and lived between UT in Austin and McDonald Observatory in West Texas.

BILL STRONG. I was an engineer at Bell Labs. I have four children, nine grandchildren, and three great grandchildren. I've lived in the Preston building for nearly four years.

MANI SUBRAMANIAN. I was born in Madras, India in 1934. My early education and employment were in India before I migrated to the US in 1959. I earned a PhD at Purdue University. My wife, Ruth, and I were married in 1964, and we have two children. Career positions include Purdue, Bell Labs, Georgia Tech, IIT Madras and Network Management Forum. Ruth and I moved to Westminster in 2020 and continue to enjoy the social and communal activities.

BOYD TAYLOR. While at UT, I studied creative writing under Gerald Langford, who was a great Faulkner scholar. As a result, I wrote with a stream-of-consciousness style for a while. That was a problem when I was practicing law, but when I turned to business, no one cared. My writing hero now is Hemingway.

MARY LIB THORNHILL. When I was six, when we were living with Papa's parents, I started painting with my aunt. I painted a storm brewing and the bending palm trees. Now at 96, I mostly work in pastel. There are over 60 of my paintings on the walls of my Westminster apartment. Painting has been a great endeavor – and sometimes quite profitable.

BETTY TYSLAN. I was born in Houston and lived in CA and PA. Playing with words, cards and Scrabble tiles are pleasant diversions. I am technologically challenged so the computer is not my friend. Westminster has been my home for over five years.

MARY LYNN WOODALL. In August, 2019, I moved to Westminster after living for forty-six years in my home in Austin, where I raised my two children, enjoyed gardening, and spending time with friends. I taught for thirty-five years at St. Andrew's Episcopal School, first as a lower school art teacher and later as the school counselor, retiring in 2014. I now enjoy the many activities offered here at Westminster.

PAUL YOUNGDALE. I am a native Texan, born in Wichita Falls, educated in the Abilene, Dallas, Austin, and Beaumont public schools. After graduation form Beaumont High School, I attended Texas Christian University where I met my wife, Patricia. We have two children and two grandsons, all living in Austin. We moved to Westminster in July, 2020.

PRINT AND DIGITAL VERSIONS
OF ALL EDITIONS
OF THE
WESTMINSTER WRITERS
JOURNAL
ARE AVAILABLE
ON AMAZON.

Made in the USA
Coppell, TX
13 January 2024

26803034R00109